Reading Advantage

Second Edition

Teacher's Guide

Casey Malarcher
Nancy Hubley

THOMSON

™

HEINLE

Australia · Canada   United States

Reading Advantage, *Second Edition*, Teacher's Guide 1
Casey Malarcher and Nancy Hubley

Publisher, Global ELT: Christopher Wenger
Editorial Manager: Sean Bermingham
Development Editor: Derek Mackrell
Production Editor: Tan Jin Hock
ELT Directors: John Lowe (Asia), Jim Goldstone (Latin America—ELT), Francisco Lozano (Latin America—Academic and Training, ELT)

Director of Marketing, ESL/ELT: Amy Mabley
Marketing Manager: Ian Martin
Cover Design: Christopher Hanzie, TYA Inc.
Interior Design and Composition: Stella Tan, TYA Inc.
Printer: Thomson/West

3   4   5   6   7   8   9   10   07   06

For more information, contact Thomson Heinle, 25 Thomson Place, Boston, Massachusetts 02210 USA, or you can visit our Internet site at http://www.heinle.com

For permission to use material from this text or product, contact us in the United States:
Tel   1-800-730-2214
Fax   1-800-730-2215
Web   www.thomsonrights.com

ISBN 1-4130-0118-1

Credits

Unless otherwise stated, all photos are from PhotoDisc, Inc. Digital Imagery © copyright 2003 PhotoDisc, Inc.

Dictionary definitions are from Heinle's *Newbury House Dictionary of American English*, © 2002, Monroe Allen Publishers, Inc.

Every effort has been made to trace all sources of illustrations/photos/information in this book, but if any have been inadvertently overlooked, the publisher will be pleased to make the necessary arrangements at the first opportunity.

Contents

About this Teacher's Guide

Reading Advantage is a high-beginner to high-intermediate series that helps adult and young adult learners build their English vocabulary and reading skills through reading passages and accompanying exercises. Each of the four levels presents twenty nonfiction passages dealing with a variety of topics. Each level of *Reading Advantage* limits the vocabulary used in readings according to a basic word list. Higher levels in the series build on the word lists established in previous levels. In addition, exercises for each unit recycle vocabulary from earlier units in the book. Thus, students are repeatedly exposed to vocabulary items throughout the book to ensure their acquisition.

This teacher's guide is divided into six sections.

Using *Reading Advantage*

This section contains a four-page walkthrough of a typical *Reading Advantage* unit. Each section of the unit is described, and suggested teaching times are given, including suggestions for longer classes. A page on Building Students' Reading Rate (page 12) addresses ways in which the teacher can become aware of, and improve, students' reading fluency. A Guide to Question Formats (page 10) describes the various question formats in the *Reading Advantage* series, and strategies students can use with each format.

Building Vocabulary

A vocabulary acquisition page describes how *Reading Advantage* addresses current theories of vocabulary acquisition, and provides references for further reading. A two-page vocabulary activity bank describes ten activities that a teacher can use in any class to practice and reinforce vocabulary. For students, there are two photocopiable sections: first, two pages of vocabulary learning tips; and, second, two pages of strategies for guessing the meaning of new vocabulary, including a list of prefixes and suffixes used in the readings in the book.

Unit Notes

For each of the twenty reading units and four review units there is a page of teacher's notes. Page 20 provides a guide to the content of each of these pages.

Unit Quizzes

This section contains twenty photocopiable unit quizzes—one for each of the units in the book.

Tests

There are two tests in this section, and an answer key. The Mid-book Test covers Units 1–10, while the Final Test covers all twenty units of the book.

Scoring Sheet and Glossary

This final section contains a photocopiable scoring sheet on which to record the score of each of your students for the twenty unit quizzes and two tests. The Glossary defines important terms related to the subjects of reading and vocabulary acquisition.

How to Teach a Unit

Each of the four books in the *Reading Advantage* series consists of twenty four-page units, with a review unit every five units. The answers and notes for the units are provided on pages 21–40.

The following sample lesson plan is provided to show teachers how units in the series can be taught in a typical 45 to 60-minute reading class. This is not the only way teachers can approach the units, and the timings are approximate—they can be lengthened or shortened according to the length of your lesson. Remember to spend a short amount of time at the beginning of each class, before opening the book, reviewing the vocabulary and reading from the previous unit. See pages 14 and 15 for activity suggestions.

▪ Before You Read (5–10 minutes)

Each unit begins with three questions for students to think about before they read the passage. The questions typically do not have right or wrong answers. They are designed to generate discussion that will bring out vocabulary or ideas useful for students in approaching the reading material. Depending on class size, the questions may be discussed as a class or in small groups.

In some cases, questions are directly answered in the reading. For example, a question may ask when a certain event occurred. In this case the teacher may tell the class, "While you are reading, see if this question is answered in the text."

Other questions, such as those that ask about student preferences or experiences, can be used for surveys of the class. The teacher can count the number of students sharing a preference or answering the same (yes or no) and record the number on the board. The results of these surveys may be compared to information presented in certain readings.

▪ Target Vocabulary (5 minutes)

In this section, students are introduced to words from the reading that may be unfamiliar to them. Students should be able to match the words with the definitions provided. The definitions give the meaning of each word in the context in which it is used in the reading passage.

After giving students time to match the vocabulary items and check the answers, it may be useful to highlight for students one or more of the following:

Part of speech: Explain how each vocabulary item is defined (as noun, verb, adjective, or adverb), and how the word can be used as another part of speech. For example, in the unit on marriage (Unit 14), the vocabulary item "date" is defined as a verb. The word may also appear as a noun without any change in form.

Irregular patterns: Certain verbs may change form completely in the past or past participle forms, such as the verb "sink, sank, sunk." Students should be aware of such irregular forms in case they appear in the reading.

Alternative meanings: Vocabulary items are defined according to usage of the items in the readings. However, certain words may appear more commonly when used with an alternative meaning. The word "couple" commonly means "few or several" (e.g., a couple of things), but in the context of the unit on marriage it means "two people who are dating." Encourage students to record common alternative definitions in their books. See pages 16 and 17 for ideas on how students can record new words in a vocabulary notebook.

Ideas for presenting and practicing vocabulary can be found in the Vocabulary Activity Bank on pages 14 and 15. Information about parts of speech and alternative meanings can be found in the Language Notes section of the Unit Notes.

Reading Passage (5 minutes)

The reading passage and exercises should typically be done together.

Have students time their first reading of the passage, and then record their time at the foot of the reading and also at the back of the Student Book. See page 12 for further guidance on using timed readings to develop students' reading fluency.

Target vocabulary items are set in **bold** to enable students to see them at a glance.

If students have any questions about the text, ask them to wait until everyone has finished reading the passage silently, and has written down their reading time. If there are words that students don't know the meaning of, don't supply the definitions at this time, but write them on the board and return to them later.

Some of the reading comprehension questions in the series involve having students guess the meaning of unknown words from context. Encourage students to practice guessing the meaning of new words from context—rather than using their dictionaries—by requiring them to keep their dictionaries closed until after they have completed the reading comprehension questions. For more information on guessing the meaning of new vocabulary, see the photocopiable guide on page 18.

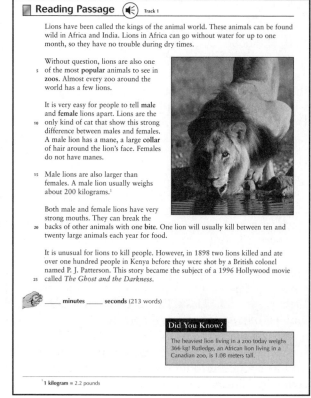

> **Reading Passage** 🔊 Track 1
>
> Lions have been called the kings of the animal world. These animals can be found wild in Africa and India. Lions in Africa can go without water for up to one month, so they have no trouble during dry times.
>
> 5 Without question, lions are also one of the most **popular** animals to see in **zoos**. Almost every zoo around the world has a few lions.
>
> It is very easy for people to tell **male** and **female** lions apart. Lions are the 10 only kind of cat that show this strong difference between males and females. A male lion has a mane, a large **collar** of hair around the lion's face. Females do not have manes.
>
> 15 Male lions are also larger than females. A male lion usually weighs about 200 kilograms.[1]
>
> Both male and female lions have very strong mouths. They can break the 20 backs of other animals with one **bite**. One lion will usually kill between ten and twenty large animals each year for food.
>
> It is unusual for lions to kill people. However, in 1898 two lions killed and ate over one hundred people in Kenya before they were shot by a British colonel named P. J. Patterson. This story became the subject of a 1996 Hollywood movie 25 called *The Ghost and the Darkness*.
>
> _____ minutes _____ seconds (213 words)
>
> **Did You Know?**
> The heaviest lion living in a zoo today weighs 366 kg! Rutledge, an African lion living in a Canadian zoo, is 1.08 meters tall.
>
> [1] **1 kilogram** = 2.2 pounds

Line numbers are provided on the left of the passage to help students refer to specific lines in the reading.

The majority of new words in the unit are assigned as target vocabulary for that unit and introduced on the first page of the unit. When additional new vocabulary needs to be included in a reading, the meanings are given in footnotes at the bottom of the page. This vocabulary is intended to be used for understanding of the passage only. These items are not tested in the review units.

The *Did You Know?* box provides an additional short interesting fact related to the reading. Encourage students to read this silently, or alternatively have a student read it aloud. This fact could be used as the starting point of a discussion. Further background notes are given in the Unit Notes (pages 21–40).

Then have students listen to the audio recording of the passage to check the pronunciation of new words. Track numbers are given at the top of the page.

Reading Comprehension Questions (5–10 minutes)

This section includes five multiple-choice questions that cover the content of the passage in a variety of ways. Some questions focus on specific details within the text, while others ask about the overall theme of the passage, and others require students to infer information that isn't stated specifically in the passage. For more information on the different types of multiple-choice questions used in *Reading Advantage*, see pages 10–11.

The questions in this section can be completed individually, or by students in pairs or small groups. Answering the questions individually will allow you to determine the abilities of individual students, but on the other hand, answering in pairs or groups will encourage communication between students, and will provide support for weaker learners.

Students may refer back to the reading when answering the questions. Once all of the students have had time to complete the comprehension questions, check the answers as a class. To check the answers, have the class respond as a group with each answer or call on individuals to give the answers. Always check to see if everyone in the class agrees. In cases where students disagree on an answer, ask students to explain how information in the reading supports their answers. If the answer is wrong, explain where the correct answer is supported in the reading. (Answers may be found on pages 21–40 of this Teacher's Guide.)

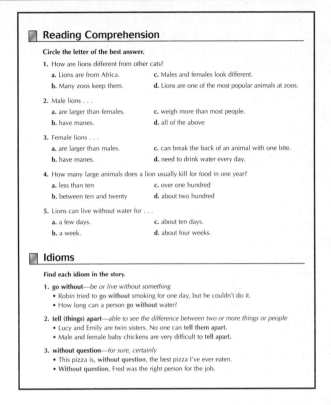

Reading Comprehension

Circle the letter of the best answer.

1. How are lions different from other cats?
   a. Lions are from Africa.
   b. Many zoos keep them.
   c. Males and females look different.
   d. Lions are one of the most popular animals at zoos.

2. Male lions . . .
   a. are larger than females.
   b. have manes.
   c. weigh more than most people.
   d. all of the above

3. Female lions . . .
   a. are larger than males.
   b. have manes.
   c. can break the back of an animal with one bite.
   d. need to drink water every day.

4. How many large animals does a lion usually kill for food in one year?
   a. less than ten
   b. between ten and twenty
   c. over one hundred
   d. about two hundred

5. Lions can live without water for . . .
   a. a few days.
   b. a week.
   c. about ten days.
   d. about four weeks.

Idioms

Find each idiom in the story.

1. go without—*be or live without something*
   • Robin tried to go without smoking for one day, but he couldn't do it.
   • How long can a person go without water?

2. tell (things) apart—*able to see the difference between two or more things or people*
   • Lucy and Emily are twin sisters. No one can tell them apart.
   • Male and female baby chickens are very difficult to tell apart.

3. without question—*for sure, certainly*
   • This pizza is, without question, the best pizza I've ever eaten.
   • Without question, Fred was the right person for the job.

Idioms (5 minutes)

Three idioms used in each passage are included in this section. The meaning of each idiom and examples of how the idiom may be used are presented here. The line in the passage in which each idiom occurs is given in the Unit Summary box of the Unit Notes (see pages 21–40).

Review the idiom definitions and examples. Provide additional examples for students when necessary. Encourage students to provide their own examples by eliciting example sentences from the class.

Have students scan the reading again to find where each idiom is used. For teachers using the audio recordings of the readings, play the recording for the class. As students listen, they can underline the idioms in the text.

> **Note:** At this point, teachers may wish to take a few minutes to allow students to ask questions regarding vocabulary or difficult sentence structures in the reading. This is also a good time to check comprehension of specific vocabulary items not covered elsewhere in the unit.

Ideas for presenting and practicing idioms are included in the Vocabulary Activity Bank on pages 14 and 15. There are several different ways in which students can record idioms in their notebooks, such as drawing pictures, grouping by similar meanings, or grouping by the same verb (e.g., *take*, *get*, *keep*). For more information on recording vocabulary see the photocopiable Vocabulary Learning Tips on pages 16 and 17.

Vocabulary Reinforcement (5 minutes)

This section includes two parts for vocabulary and idiom practice. Words and idioms in this section may come from the current unit or previous units. The first part of the section contains six multiple-choice questions in two formats. Students must either choose the best word from the choices to fill a blank in the sentence, or they need to choose a word from the choices that means the same as the word written in *italics* in the question. The second part of the section is a cloze passage, where learners read the passage and find items from the box to fill in the blanks. Explain to students that one word in the box is extra (i.e., not needed). For more information on the different types of Vocabulary Reinforcement questions used in *Reading Advantage*, see pages 10–11.

Allow students time to answer on their own. Have students work in pairs to check their answers. As a class, go over each item to make sure everyone has the correct answers.

What Do You Think? (5–10 minutes)

Students are encouraged here to think further about what they have read and to communicate their own ideas and opinions about the topics presented.

Depending on class size, the questions presented in this part of the unit may be discussed as a class or in small groups. The questions typically do not have right or wrong answers. They are designed to generate discussion. Encourage students to ask follow-up questions in their groups rather than just limiting themselves to answering the questions in the book.

In the case where students first discuss in small groups, have one member of each group report to the class one interesting point the group discussed.

In addition, or as an alternative, the questions can be used as the basis of a writing activity. See the Unit Notes (pages 21–40) for further writing activity suggestions.

General Tips

- *Don't ask, "What does ___ mean?"* It is easier for students to provide a word for a given definition rather than to define a word. Therefore, instead of asking students, "What does <u>zoo</u> mean?", give the definition yourself by asking, "Which word in the text means <u>a place where animals are kept to look at</u>?"

- *Put words on the board for students to see.* During pre-reading discussion, students can come up with words related to the reading which are not listed as vocabulary items for the unit. Write these words on the board and leave them up during the class. Such words can be useful to students later, especially during the discussion at the end of class. Be sure to add these words to the Vocabulary Box (see page 15) for recycling.

- *Don't make students read aloud the first time they read the passage.* The first time students read the passage they should read silently and record their reading speed. When students read aloud they are less likely to achieve their natural reading speed, and they are likely to be worrying more about the pronunciation of the reading, than the meaning. If you like to have students read aloud in your class, after the Idioms or Vocabulary Reinforcement section would be a suitable time.

Suggestions for Longer Classes

If you have classes longer than 60 minutes and need additional material, see:

- the Unit Quizzes on pages 46–65;
- listening and speaking activities in the Unit Notes (pages 21–40);
- writing extension ideas in the Unit Notes;
- extension activities for the Review Units (pages 41–44).

Guide to Question Formats

A variety of question forms come up in the *Reading Advantage* series. If you gradually introduce the skills required to answer each type of question as they appear in *Reading Advantage* and encourage students to practice them consistently, you will foster good habits that will reward your students with better examination performance. Many of the question formats used in *Reading Advantage* are similar to those used in standardized exams.

Multiple-Choice Questions

Multiple-choice questions are popular because they are versatile, objective, and easy to mark. They are used in *Reading Advantage* for a range of question types, in the Reading Comprehension and Vocabulary Reinforcement sections, as well as Review Units and Quizzes. Here are some varieties of multiple-choice questions:

Specific Details

The simplest type asks for specific information from the reading passage, for example, "Where was Thomas Adams from?"

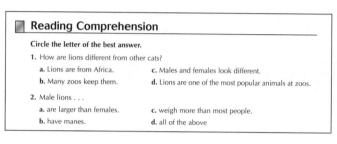

Reading Comprehension

Circle the letter of the best answer.

1. How are lions different from other cats?
   a. Lions are from Africa.
   b. Many zoos keep them.
   c. Males and females look different.
   d. Lions are one of the most popular animals at zoos.

2. Male lions . . .
   a. are larger than females.
   b. have manes.
   c. weigh more than most people.
   d. all of the above

Negative Statements

A question frequently found in the Reading Comprehension section is "Which of these sentences is NOT true?" Sometimes the best way to answer this is to eliminate the answers that ARE true. In other words, if students can find support for the true answers in the reading passage, then they know that those options are not the answer. Note that students need to occasionally watch out for double negatives—where there is a negative in both the question stem and the option, for example, "What is NOT true about blood type AB? . . . b. It is not the most common type." (Unit 18)

Main Ideas

Multiple-choice questions are often used to test comprehension of main ideas either at the paragraph or whole text level. A common approach to main idea questions is that the correct option is at just the right level of specificity whereas the distractors are too specific, too general, or off topic. Main idea questions are sometimes worded as "Choose the best title."

Inference

The most difficult type of multiple-choice question in *Reading Advantage* is inference questions, which require students to go beyond what is literally given and draw conclusions, for example, "Which team probably surprised the most people in the 2002 World Cup?"

All, every, and none: Sometimes the answer options will include *all of the above* or *none of the above*. When this happens, all or none of the other three options would work in order for the option to be selected.

True, False, or Unknown

This format, used in unit quizzes and tests, is used to help students clarify what is actually stated in the paragraph, what is paraphrased or implied, and what is not given or provided. This format is especially useful for discerning fact from opinion. Here are some simple guidelines to using this format:

the birthday party, it turned into a picnic by candlelight because the city went without electricity for several days. Sam said he'd never forget it.

A. Read the passage and decide if the statement is *true, false,* or *unknown*. Circle your answer.

31. true	false	unknown	A *blackout* means it is dark without electric lights.
32. true	false	unknown	People in seven northwestern states had a problem.
33. true	false	unknown	Elevators and subways did not run, but airports worked as usual.
34. true	false	unknown	Kim works for a publisher on the 70th floor of the tower.
35. true	false	unknown	Kim had to walk down 65 floors of stairs.

True information is given in the passage but it is often paraphrased, or said in other words. Train students to look for similar *meaning*, not exact words. In *Reading Advantage*, vocabulary is often recycled by using synonyms to stretch the students' active vocabulary.

If the statement is **false**, students can find the correct information in the passage and fix the statement. When you give back quizzes, encourage students to do this.

Unknown means the information is not found in the passage. When students bring background knowledge to reading a passage, sometimes they think they've read something that isn't actually included.

Matching

Every unit in *Reading Advantage* has several matching exercises, for example, in the Target Vocabulary section. Get students into the habit of crossing out items as they use them so they don't use the same item twice. Also, encourage them to move on to other questions if there is one that is difficult at first. When they have finished the others, there

> **Match each word with the best meaning.**
>
> 1. _____ bite   **a.** material around the neck (e.g., on a shirt or dress)
> 2. _____ male   **b.** to cut with the teeth
> 3. _____ female   **c.** boy or man
> 4. _____ collar   **d.** a place where animals are kept for people to look at
> 5. _____ popular   **e.** girl or woman
> 6. _____ zoo   **f.** well-liked by many people

will be fewer options left and perhaps they will be able to make a good choice. In most *Reading Advantage* matching exercises and quiz sections, each item is used only once and there are extra items that are not used.

Cloze and Gap Fill

In the Vocabulary Reinforcement section there are both gap fill (section A) and cloze (section B) sections. Cloze exercises also occur in the *Reading Advantage* tests and quizzes. Encourage students to look at the words surrounding the gap for collocations and to think of what part of speech the word needs to be. In a few cases, students are given an initial letter for a missing word and must supply the word from memory. This is done to encourage students to produce new vocabulary as well as just recognize it. However, in the grading of unit quizzes, credit should be given if the word is recognizable even if the spelling is not exact. This follows practice on a number of standardized exams.

> **A.** Circle the letter of the word or phrase that best completes the sentence.
>
> 1. Without question, lions are my favorite animal at the _____.
>   **a.** world   **b.** king   **c.** zoo   **d.** collar
> 2. Male and female fish are hard to tell _____.
>   **a.** from   **b.** with   **c.** apart   **d.** them
> 3. Her dress had a very high _____.
>   **a.** female   **b.** collar   **c.** mane   **d.** bite

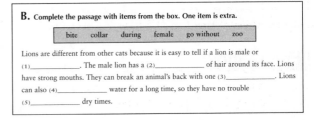

> **B.** Complete the passage with items from the box. One item is extra.
>
> | bite | collar | during | female | go without | zoo |
>
> Lions are different from other cats because it is easy to tell if a lion is male or (1)_____. The male lion has a (2)_____ of hair around its face. Lions have strong mouths. They can break an animal's back with one (3)_____. Lions can also (4)_____ water for a long time, so they have no trouble (5)_____ dry times.

Wrong Word Out

This type of question is found in the quizzes and review units. Four vocabulary items are given; three have something in common, and the fourth is different. To solve this kind of question, students need to first identify the common idea, then look for the one that doesn't match. Note

> One of the four items is different from the other three. Circle the letter of your choice.
>
> 11. **a.** terrible   **b.** dangerous   **c.** cruel   **d.** successful
> 12. **a.** marble   **b.** gloves   **c.** collar   **d.** underwear
> 13. **a.** twist   **b.** beside   **c.** lean   **d.** sink
> 14. **a.** shout   **b.** bite   **c.** bury   **d.** chew
> 15. **a.** earn   **b.** money   **c.** win   **d.** afford

that the odd word out is distinguished because of **meaning** and not for other reasons such as spelling, or the number of letters, or the pronunciation.

Building Students' Reading Rate

A major aim of the *Reading Advantage* series is to increase your students' reading rate, or reading fluency, while also ensuring accuracy. A high reading rate is essential to enjoyable extensive reading outside the classroom. It also is important for taking exams with a reading component. Here are some suggestions to make your students aware of their own reading rate, and to monitor its progress.

How to Do Timed Readings in Class

Using a watch or clock, have all students begin reading silently at the same time. To time the readings, prepare time cards to hold up for the class. Cards can be marked with five-second intervals, as five seconds, ten seconds, fifteen seconds, up to one minute forty seconds, one minute forty-five seconds, etc. When students have finished reading, they can simply look up to see their times. Have students record their reading times in the space in the book below the reading, and then in the chart on the inside back cover of the book. Note that the readings in Book 1 of *Reading Advantage* are around two hundred words long. The rates on the chart at the back of the book are based on an average passage length of 215 words. (The actual word count for each passage is noted under each reading.)

You may wish to set a class reading rate goal, for example, by taking the average reading rate at the beginning of the course and adding a certain percentage to it. For comparison, the average reading speed for U.S. college students is 200–250 words per minute, but it would be unrealistic to expect your students to achieve this speed.

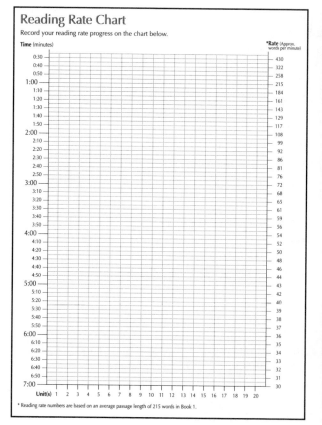

Reading Rate Chart
Record your reading rate progress on the chart below.

Time (minutes)	*Rate (Approx. words per minute)
0:30	430
0:40	322
0:50	258
1:00	215
1:10	184
1:20	161
1:30	143
1:40	129
1:50	117
2:00	108
2:10	99
2:20	92
2:30	86
2:40	81
2:50	76
3:00	72
3:10	68
3:20	65
3:30	61
3:40	59
3:50	56
4:00	54
4:10	52
4:20	50
4:30	48
4:40	46
4:50	44
5:00	43
5:10	42
5:20	40
5:30	39
5:40	38
5:50	37
6:00	36
6:10	35
6:20	34
6:30	33
6:40	32
6:50	31
7:00	30

Unit(s) 1 2 3 4 5 6 7 8 9 10 11 12 13 14 15 16 17 18 19 20

* Reading rate numbers are based on an average passage length of 215 words in Book 1.

Variations

Have students read more than once. Reading fluency can be developed through repeated reading of the same text. A good time for repeated reading is after finding idioms in the unit's reading passage, before moving on to the Vocabulary Reinforcement. At this point in the lesson, have students look back at the unit from the previous class. For example, on the day the class is doing Unit 14, have them look back at Unit 13 for repeated reading. This will help to reinforce the vocabulary for the previous unit.

Do a timed reading of the repeated text. Use the time cards to show how long students take to read the passage, and have students record their new reading time below their old time. Alternatively, set a time for the class to read (i.e., one minute or two minutes). Have students mark the place in the text they reach by the time limit. Setting a time limit for reading works well when students read a text three or four times, marking each time the point they reach by the time limit. Students will be able to see for themselves how their reading fluency is progressing.

For more background information on developing reading rate, you may wish to read *Exploring Second Language Reading: Issues and Strategies* (Neil Anderson 1999, Heinle/Thomson).

Vocabulary Acquisition

It is generally agreed that the key to success in English language learning, particularly in developing good reading skills, is vocabulary acquisition. Before we explore specific techniques and activities for helping students with vocabulary acquisition, let's look at some fundamental principles.

There are three main ways in which we acquire new vocabulary:
1. We can be deliberately taught certain words and idioms.
2. We can pick up new vocabulary through reading and speaking.
3. We can learn certain strategies which aid in guessing the meaning of new words.

All three of these methods are addressed in the *Reading Advantage* series.

In our first language, we combine these approaches after we have achieved a basic core vocabulary of the most commonly used words. For beginning and low-intermediate students to benefit from the second and third strategies, they need to control a basic vocabulary of the most frequently used words or lexical items of English. The *Reading Advantage* series aims to provide students with this core vocabulary. Gradually, as students' vocabularies enlarge, in the higher levels of the series, strategies increase in significance.

Nation (1990) says that students need to know 95 percent of the words in a passage before they can effectively use guessing strategies for the 5 percent unknown words. Anderson (1999) suggests that basic vocabulary should be explicitly taught in conjunction with teaching students other strategies for less frequently encountered items. As the *Reading Advantage* series progresses, more emphasis will be placed on inferring meaning through word structure (such as word roots, prefixes, and affixes), exploring the role that new vocabulary plays in a specific context, and developing dictionary skills. The *Reading Advantage* teacher's book contains photocopiable vocabulary learning tips (pages 16 and 17) and a guide to guessing the meaning of new vocabulary (page 18), including a list of suffixes and prefixes in the book.

Research has suggested that it takes an average of at least seven encounters with a vocabulary item for it to be remembered. To help students remember vocabulary, an important characteristic of *Reading Advantage* is its focus on vocabulary recycling. Throughout the book, vocabulary is recycled not only in subsequent passages, but also in the vocabulary reinforcement sections, the unit quizzes, review units, and tests.

Further Reading

For teachers interested in the theory and practice of vocabulary acquisition, the list below will provide a good starting point.

Anderson, Neil (1999), *Exploring Second Language Reading: Issues and Strategies*, Heinle/Thomson

Flower, John (1994), *Phrasal Verb Organiser with Mini-Dictionary*, Language Teaching Publications/Thomson

Gough, Chris (2000), *English Vocabulary Organiser*, Language Teaching Publications/Thomson

Lewis, Michael (Editor) (2000), *Teaching Collocation*, Language Teaching Publications/Thomson

Nation, I. S. P. (1990), *Teaching and Learning Vocabulary*, Heinle/Thomson

Nation, I. S. P. (2001), *Learning Vocabulary in Another Language*, Cambridge University Press

Schmitt, Norbert (2000), *Vocabulary in Language Teaching*, Cambridge University Press

Wright, Jon (1999), *Idioms Organizer*, Language Teaching Publications/Thomson

Vocabulary Activity Bank

Below are ten activities you can use in class to present and practice vocabulary. Here are some general tips:

- Go over the instructions carefully. Stop the class and explain again if there seem to be problems.
- Use a variety of group sizes. Sometimes have students work as individuals.
- Whenever possible, make the activities learner-centered, for example by having groups work in smaller groups rather than as a class, or by choosing a student to take the role of the teacher and conduct the activity.
- Mix language skills and types of activities to cater to different learning styles.
- Create a manageable number of groups so that you can circulate and monitor.

1 Hangman

This old favorite promotes both fluency and accuracy. Divide the class into two competing teams who take turns presenting and answering vocabulary questions. The presenting team draws short lines on the board, each line representing a letter in a word. The goal is for the other team to guess the answer correctly before ten tries "hangs" them. Each incorrect guess becomes one more line on a graphic drawn on the board. Start numbering from the base.

Scoring can be done in several ways. When a team answers correctly within the limits, they get one point and they present next. If they can't answer within ten tries, the presenting team gets five points and another turn to present. The traditional diagram for this game is a person hanging, but if this image makes you or your students uncomfortable, then use another illustration, such as the spider, instead.

2 Bingo

The goal of Bingo is to form a straight line of five squares on a board of five squares across by five squares down. Lines can be made horizontally, vertically, or diagonally.

To start, either hand out blank grids, or ask students to draw them on a blank piece of paper. The game works best when the vocabulary is limited to a common set of words, such as words and idioms from the last five units. Have students write words in the boxes without looking at other students' cards. A leader (this may be the teacher, or it can be other students) then calls out definitions, synonyms, antonyms, or examples of words. Students mark a box if they have the word. The first to get a straight run calls BINGO and is the winner. If you have a large class and want to allow discussion, you can have more than one student per card.

3 Word Strings

Have the class form a circle. Say a word. The next person has to say a different word that starts with the last letter of the previous word. No repeats are allowed, so students must listen carefully. This game focuses students' attention on the spelling and pronunciation of word beginnings and endings (especially reduced forms and homonyms such as *threw/through*).

4 Balderdash/Call My Bluff

Write ten items on small pieces of paper and fold the papers. Divide the class into ten groups and have each group select one piece of paper. Each group then writes three definitions for the item on their paper, of which only one is correct. Teams then take turns presenting their definitions to the rest of the class. The first team to identify a false definition gets a point—if they can provide a correct definition. In order for a team to win the point, the definition must be corrected. If a team identifies a correct definition as incorrect, then their team loses a point.

5   Idiom Charades

Choose fifteen vocabulary items—this game is easiest with idioms—and write them on pieces of card, one for each card. Number the cards. Have students work in pairs, each pair drawing a card. The pair has two minutes to think how to act out the idiom without speaking. The pairs act out their idioms in order, with the ones holding card one going first. Appoint a timekeeper. If the class can guess the idiom within a minute, the presenting pair gets a point.

6   Memory Test

Take sixteen identical small pieces of card for each group of five to seven players. Distribute the blank cards to each group. Assign a unit to the group and ask them to write eight new vocabulary items or idioms on the cards. They then write synonyms on the other eight cards. Have each group pass their set of cards to another group. Have a student in each group shuffle the cards and place them face down on a table in four rows of four cards. Each student picks up two cards. If they match, s/he may keep them. If they don't, the cards are replaced, face down, and another student takes a turn. This continues until all pairs of cards are identified. The person with the most cards is the winner. Time permitting, groups can exchange cards with each other.

This game is sometimes known as *Pelmanism*.

7   Picture Hunt

In this game, teams race to find examples of words starting with particular letters in a picture or photo dictionary. Use categories where there are large sets of examples, such as food, clothing, classroom items, etc. The team tries to find items starting with each letter of the alphabet. The winner is the team that completes the alphabet first or has the greatest number of examples.

8   Twenty Questions

In this game, students choose a card from the Vocabulary Box, and keep the word on it secret from the rest of the class. The other students try to guess the item by asking questions that can be answered with "yes" or "no." For example: Is the word an adjective? Does it start with *sch*? Does it have three syllables? Does it mean the same thing as "horrible"? If someone gets the answer within twenty questions they get a point and a chance to present the next word. If the answer is not guessed within twenty questions, the presenter gets five points and another turn.

The Vocabulary Box

A good technique for choosing vocabulary to be reviewed is to use a Vocabulary Box. As new vocabulary items arise in the lesson, write them on the board. At the end of the lesson write each item on a separate small piece of paper, and then put these pieces of paper in a cardboard box. Whenever you have time in a lesson for vocabulary review, choose cards at random from this box to provide items for review. Review the words regularly by asking students for definitions, spelling, synonyms, or use in sentences. Over a period of weeks, as students come to know an item thoroughly, it can be removed from the box.

9   Writing and Acting Scripts

Divide students into small groups. Provide each group with a list of vocabulary items, or cards from the Vocabulary Box. Ten items for each group would be enough. Make sure each group has different words. Have groups work together to create a short dialogue or play which includes all the words on their list. When they are finished, have them act their dialogue out for the class. See Review Activities 11–15 (page 43) for more information.

10   Defining and Guessing in Pairs

Provide students with a list of words. Students work in pairs, and take turns defining their word to their partner, without using the word itself. See Review Activities Units 16–20 (page 44) for more information.

In addition to these activity ideas you may wish to adapt some of the vocabulary learning techniques on pages 16–17, for use as classroom activities. For example, provide students with a vocabulary item or theme from one of the units, and have them work in groups to create a Word Map of associated items. See Review Activities Units 1–5 (page 41) for more information.

Vocabulary Learning Tips

The one best thing you can do to improve your English is to increase your vocabulary. Here are some suggestions:

◨ Keep a Vocabulary Notebook

Buy a notebook and write down new words and idioms that you want to remember. There are different ways of organizing your notebook. Here are some suggestions:

a) Label pictures

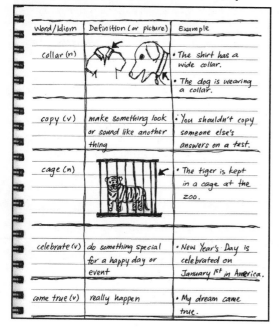

b) Word maps

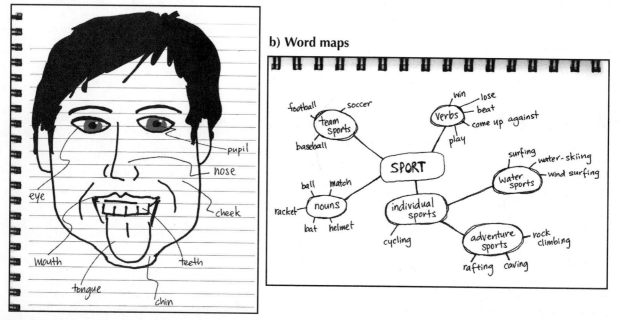

c) List words with definitions and examples

Word/Idiom	Definition (or picture)	Example
collar (n)		• The shirt has a wide collar. • The dog is wearing a collar.
copy (v)	make something look or sound like another thing	• You shouldn't copy someone else's answers on a test.
cage (n)		• The tiger is kept in a cage at the zoo.
celebrate (v)	do something special for a happy day or event	• New Year's Day is celebrated on January 1st in America.
come true (v)	really happen	• My dream came true.

d) Note words that go together—*collocations*

take go on need have	a	long two-week short summer school	vacation	next week in Italy with my family by myself

announce attend cancel hold organize	a(n)	exciting (in)formal important historic shocking unique	event	took place occurred happened

Use Flashcards

Flashcards are a great way to learn new vocabulary. Make them on thick paper by cutting the paper into cards of the same size. Here is an example of a flashcard:

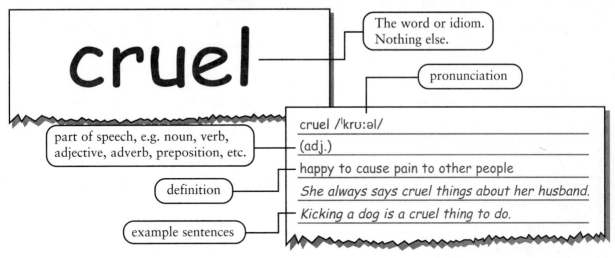

Your flashcards might look the same as this, or they might have more information. Other things you can write on the back of your flashcards are: pictures, translations in your own language, opposites, words that mean the same, and memory aids (see Other Tips).

Remember: Carry your flashcards around with you and when you have free time, look at them and test yourself. You can use them alone, or with a friend. Exchange flashcards with a friend and test each other!

Other Tips

Read, read, read One of the best ways to enlarge your English vocabulary is to read for fun. Read (easy) magazines and books in English outside class. The best place to start is with Graded Readers. Ask your teacher for some suggestions.

Use an English/English dictionary To learn more about new words in your notebook, use a dictionary. Try to find an English/English dictionary that's written for learners. One example is *Heinle's Basic Newbury House Dictionary of American English*. In addition to the meaning of the word, a good dictionary for learners should show you other information such as the pronunciation, the part of speech, and example sentences.

Keep a list of prefixes and suffixes In your notebook, keep lists of prefixes and suffixes and their meanings (see page 19). Make lists of words that contain the same prefix or suffix.

Label things Put small signs or labels on common, everyday things around your home.

Use memory aids A memory aid (also called a *mnemonic*) is a way of remembering a word by making a connection in your brain. For example, if you want to learn the idiom *keep an eye on someone,* meaning "to watch someone carefully," you might picture someone holding *an eye* and putting it on someone's shoulder, so they can watch them carefully. The stranger the picture is, the more you will remember it!

Another memory aid is to find a word in your own language that sounds like the new English word and make a connection. For example: a Japanese student learning the English word *knee*, meaning *the joint in your leg*, might think that *knee* sounds like the Japanese word *ni*, meaning *two*. She could then picture someone with *two large knees*. Remember to make the picture unusual to make it easier to remember. Picture two really, really big knees! Try to find English words that sound like words in your own language.

Guessing the Meaning of New Vocabulary

No one knows all the words they come across. Even native speakers often find unknown words. Of course, as you build your vocabulary, you'll know more words. In the meantime, here's a strategy or plan that you can use to guess the meaning of the new words. Follow the steps 1–5.

1. **Even if you can't understand the word, can you understand the rest of the sentence?**

   *Example: The man ran **snorkily** to the top of the hill, and then ran down the other side.*

   In this sentence *snorkily* is an unknown word (it is not a real word). You can see that it is probably an adverb because it follows a verb (*ran*) and ends in *-ily*, but you don't know what it means. However, you don't need to know what it means to understand the idea of the sentence. Keep reading the rest of the passage and come back to the word when you've finished. Remember, you don't have to understand every word to understand the meaning of a passage.

   If you need to know the meaning of the word to understand the passage, try the next strategy.

2. **Can you guess the meaning of the word from the other words in the sentence, or from the sentences before and after?**

   *Example: I climbed up on the horse and sat on the **saddle** and then picked up the **reins**. We started to ride!*

   In this sentence there are two new words, *saddle* and *reins*. From the sentence you can see that a saddle is a noun because it follows the word *the*, and has the word *and* after it. Also, you can tell it is something that you can sit on, and it is on a horse. From this you can guess that *saddle* is the name of the seat on a horse (correct).

   Reins is more difficult. Again, you know it is a noun because it follows the word *the* and is followed by a period. Also, because it ends with *-s* it is probably plural. You can tell from the sentence that they are something you can pick up, and they are probably connected to a horse, so you can guess they are the pieces of rope or leather used to control a horse (correct) but you aren't completely sure. However, you can still understand the sentence without understanding the word, so keep reading the passage.

3. **Is the meaning of the word given in the sentence?**

   *Example: Last night I bought some great **pumpernickel**, a kind of dark bread.*

   In this sentence, the word *pumpernickel* is a new word. Look at the words after the comma, "a kind of dark bread." This is the definition of *pumpernickel*. Here are some other ways in which definitions may be given in the sentence:

   *Here is a **strategy** or plan that you can use to guess the meaning of new words.*
   (*Strategy* is a noun that has a similar meaning to *plan*.)

   *Light and dark are **antonyms** (opposites).*
   (*Antonym* is a noun that means "opposite.")

   *The number of **vegetarians**—people who don't eat meat—is growing every year.*
   ("People who don't eat meat" is the definition of *vegetarians*, so a *vegetarian* is "a person who doesn't eat meat.")

4. **Can you see a word you know inside the unknown word?**

   *Example: That shop sells expensive **underwear**.*

   In this sentence *underwear* is the unknown word. You know that *underwear* is a noun (it follows the adjective *expensive*). You also know that it is something that a shop sells, and that it can be expensive. Look at the word *underwear* carefully. You can see that it contains the words *under* and *wear*. From this you can guess that it is something that you wear, and that it is something that goes under. You can guess that *underwear* is the word for clothes you wear under your other clothes.

   Be careful—this strategy doesn't always work (for example, *understand* doesn't mean "to stand under something"), but it is often useful.

5. **Does the word have any prefixes and suffixes that can help you?**

   *Example: The students in the class were **uncontrollable**.*

   With the word *uncontrollable* in this sentence, you can't tell exactly what part of speech it is. It could be a noun (e.g. *The students were girls.*); it could be an adjective (e.g. *The students were young.*); or it could be a verb (e.g. *The students were hit.*).

However, if you look at *uncontrollable* carefully, you can see the word *control* inside. Perhaps it has the meaning of control. After *control* you can see the **suffix** *-able*, which means "able to be," so *controllable* means "able to be controlled." Then, you can see the **prefix** *un-*, which means "not" or "the opposite meaning," before the word *controllable*. So, you now know that *uncontrollable* means "can't be controlled."

Here are some more examples:

*This new glass is **unbreakable**.*
(It can't be broken.)

*The bus was full of **preschoolers**.*
(*Pre-* means "before," *-er* means "someone or someone who is or does something," *-s* makes the plural of most nouns. *Preschoolers* are young children who don't go to school yet.)

Here is a list of prefixes and suffixes that appear in the reading passages of *Reading Advantage Book 1.*

Prefixes

Prefix	Meaning	Examples
centi-	a hundredth ($^1/_{100}$)	centimeter
co-	doing something together	coworker
dis-	the opposite	disappear, discover
ex-	before, but not now	ex-wife
kilo-	a thousand	kilogram, kilometer
milli-	a thousandth ($^1/_{1000}$)	millimeter
re-	again	remarry
un-	not, the opposite meaning	unusual, unsuccessful
vice-	second-most important	vice-president

Suffixes

Suffix	Meaning	Examples
-al	used to make an adjective from a noun	traditional, original
-an / -ian	added to a place name to mean "from that place", added to a famous person's name to mean "following the ideas of that person"	American, Roman, Christian
-ence / -ance	added to some adjectives to make a noun	difference
-er	(after an adjective) more	smaller
-er / -or	someone or something that does something	teacher, visitor
-ess	sometimes used instead of *-er* or *-or* for women. Sounds old-fashioned.	actress
-est	the most (added to an adjective)	oldest, fastest
-ful	full of, containing	successful, beautiful
-ion / -sion / -tion	used to make a noun from a verb	competition
-ish	added to some place names to mean "from that place"	Turkish
-ist	a person who does a kind of work	artist, scientist
-ity	used to make a noun from an adjective	popularity
-ize / -ise	used to make a verb from an adjective or noun, "to become or to make something ___"	standardized
-ly	used to make an adverb from an adjective	completely, slowly
-ous	used to make an adjective from a noun	dangerous, famous
-wide	all over a place	worldwide

Note: The rules about using suffixes are complicated. Words that use them should be learned case by case.

Introduction to Unit Notes

For each of the twenty units in *Reading Advantage*, there is a page of notes.

Answers to the Target Vocabulary, Reading Comprehension, and Vocabulary Reinforcement questions

The **Unit Summary** lists the target vocabulary and idioms for that unit. The number of the line on which each idiom first occurs is provided in parentheses after the idiom.

The **Listening and Speaking Extension** provides an activity related to the theme of the unit to provide in-class speaking practice. If you don't want to practice speaking with your class, many of these activities could be modified for homework writing tasks.

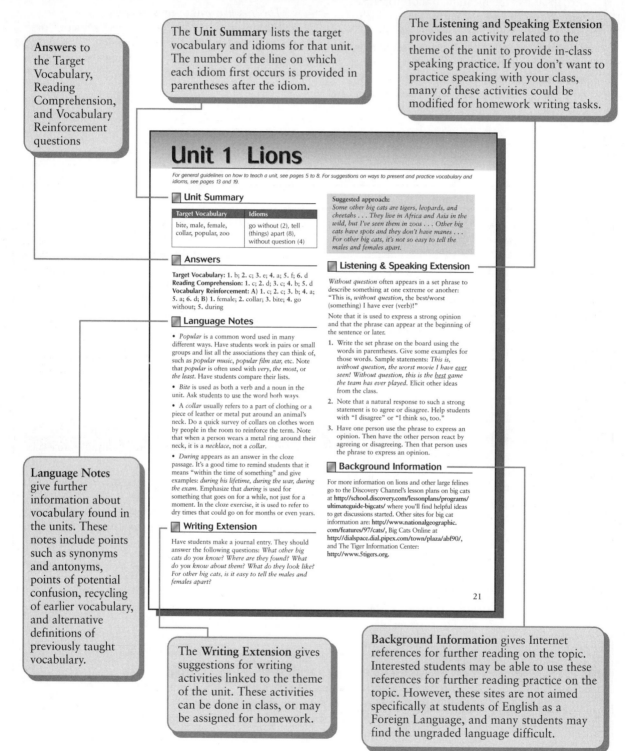

Unit 1 Lions

For general guidelines on how to teach a unit, see pages 5 to 8. For suggestions on ways to present and practice vocabulary and idioms, see pages 13 and 19.

Unit Summary

Target Vocabulary	Idioms
bite, male, female, collar, popular, zoo	go without (2), tell (things) apart (8), without question (4)

Answers

Target Vocabulary: 1. b; 2. c; 3. e; 4. a; 5. f; 6. d
Reading Comprehension: 1. c; 2. d; 3. c; 4. b; 5. d
Vocabulary Reinforcement: A) 1. c; 2. c; 3. b; 4. a; 5. a; 6. d; B) 1. female; 2. collar; 3. bite; 4. go without; 5. during

Language Notes

- *Popular* is a common word used in many different ways. Have students work in pairs or small groups and list all the associations they can think of, such as *popular music, popular film star,* etc. Note that *popular* is often used with *very, the most,* or *the least.* Have students compare their lists.
- *Bite* is used as both a verb and a noun in the unit. Ask students to use the word both ways.
- A *collar* usually refers to a part of clothing or a piece of leather or metal put around an animal's neck. Do a quick survey of collars on clothes worn by people in the room to reinforce the term. Note that when a person wears a metal ring around their neck, it is a *necklace,* not a *collar.*
- *During* appears as an answer in the cloze passage. It's a good time to remind students that it means "within the time of something" and give examples: *during his lifetime, during the war, during the exam.* Emphasize that *during* is used for something that goes on for a while, not just for a moment. In the cloze exercise, it is used to refer to dry times that could go on for months or even years.

Writing Extension

Have students make a journal entry. They should answer the following questions: *What other big cats do you know? Where are they found? What do you know about them? What do they look like? For other big cats, is it easy to tell the males and females apart?*

Suggested approach:
Some other big cats are tigers, leopards, and cheetahs . . . They live in Africa and Asia in the wild, but I've seen them in zoos . . . Other big cats have spots and they don't have manes . . . For other big cats, it's not so easy to tell the males and females apart.

Listening & Speaking Extension

Without question often appears in a set phrase to describe something at one extreme or another: "This is, *without question,* the best/worst (something) I have ever (verb)!"

Note that it is used to express a strong opinion and that the phrase can appear at the beginning of the sentence or later.

1. Write the set phrase on the board using the words in parentheses. Give some examples for those words. Sample statements: *This is, without question, the worst movie I have ever seen! Without question, this is the best game the team has ever played.* Elicit other ideas from the class.

2. Note that a natural response to such a strong statement is to agree or disagree. Help students with "I disagree" or "I think so, too."

3. Have one person use the phrase to express an opinion. Then have the other person react by agreeing or disagreeing. Then that person uses the phrase to express an opinion.

Background Information

For more information on lions and other large felines go to the Discovery Channel's lesson plans on big cats at http://school.discovery.com/lessonplans/programs/ultimateguide-bigcats/ where you'll find helpful ideas to get discussions started. Other sites for big cat information are: http://www.nationalgeographic.com/features/97/cats/, Big Cats Online at http://dialspace.dial.pipex.com/town/plaza/abf90/, and The Tiger Information Center: http://www.5tigers.org.

21

Language Notes give further information about vocabulary found in the units. These notes include points such as synonyms and antonyms, points of potential confusion, recycling of earlier vocabulary, and alternative definitions of previously taught vocabulary.

The **Writing Extension** gives suggestions for writing activities linked to the theme of the unit. These activities can be done in class, or may be assigned for homework.

Background Information gives Internet references for further reading on the topic. Interested students may be able to use these references for further reading practice on the topic. However, these sites are not aimed specifically at students of English as a Foreign Language, and many students may find the ungraded language difficult.

There is also a page of notes for each of the four review units (pages 41–44). Each review unit notes page contains the answers for the review activities, as well as a suggested extension activity.

Unit 1 Lions

For general guidelines on how to teach a unit, see pages 5 to 8. For suggestions on ways to present and practice vocabulary and idioms, see pages 13 to 19.

Unit Summary

Target Vocabulary	Idioms
bite, male, female, collar, popular, zoo	go without (2), tell (things) apart (8), without question (4)

Answers

Target Vocabulary: 1. b; 2. c; 3. e; 4. a; 5. f; 6. d
Reading Comprehension: 1. c; 2. d; 3. c; 4. b; 5. d
Vocabulary Reinforcement: A) 1. c; 2. c; 3. b; 4. a; 5. a; 6. d; **B)** 1. female; 2. collar; 3. bite; 4. go without; 5. during

Language Notes

• *Popular* is a common word used in many different ways. Have students work in pairs or small groups and list all the associations they can think of, such as *popular music, popular film star,* etc. Note that *popular* is often used with *very, the most,* or *the least.* Have students compare their lists.

• *Bite* is used as both a verb and a noun in the unit. Ask students to use the word both ways.

• A *collar* usually refers to a part of clothing or a piece of leather or metal put around an animal's neck. Do a quick survey of collars on clothes worn by people in the room to reinforce the term. Note that when a person wears a metal ring around their neck, it is a *necklace,* not a *collar.*

• *During* appears as an answer in the cloze passage. It's a good time to remind students that it means "within the time of something" and give examples: *during his lifetime, during the war, during the exam.* Emphasize that *during* is used for something that goes on for a while, not just for a moment. In the cloze exercise, it is used to refer to dry times that could go on for months or even years.

Writing Extension

Have students make a journal entry. They should answer the following questions: *What other big cats do you know? Where are they found? What do you know about them? What do they look like? For other big cats, is it easy to tell the males and females apart?*

Suggested approach:
Some other big cats are tigers, leopards, and cheetahs . . . They live in Africa and Asia in the wild, but I've seen them in zoos . . . Other big cats have spots and they don't have manes . . . For other big cats, it's not so easy to tell the males and females apart.

Listening & Speaking Extension

Without question often appears in a set phrase to describe something at one extreme or another: "This is, *without question,* the best/worst (something) I have ever (verb)!"

Note that it is used to express a strong opinion and that the phrase can appear at the beginning of the sentence or later.

1. Write the set phrase on the board using the words in parentheses. Give some examples for those words. Sample statements: *This is, without question, the worst movie I have ever seen! Without question, this is the best game the team has ever played.* Elicit other ideas from the class.

2. Note that a natural response to such a strong statement is to agree or disagree. Help students with "I disagree" or "I think so, too."

3. Have one person use the phrase to express an opinion. Then have the other person react by agreeing or disagreeing. Then that person uses the phrase to express an opinion.

Background Information

For more information on lions and other large felines go to the Discovery Channel's lesson plans on big cats at **http://school.discovery.com/lessonplans/programs/ultimateguide-bigcats/** where you'll find helpful ideas to get discussions started. Other sites for big cat information are: **http://www.nationalgeographic.com/features/97/cats/,** Big Cats Online at **http://dialspace.dial.pipex.com/town/plaza/abf90/,** and The Tiger Information Center: **http://www.5tigers.org.**

Unit 2 Harry Potter

For general guidelines on how to teach a unit, see pages 5 to 8. For suggestions on ways to present and practice vocabulary and idioms, see pages 13 to 19.

Unit Summary

Target Vocabulary	Idioms
publish, translate, earn, afford, apartment, successful	a number of (3), take off (10), around the world (19)

Answers

Target Vocabulary: 1. c; 2. f; 3. b; 4. e; 5. a; 6. d
Reading Comprehension: 1. c; 2. c; 3. b; 4. a; 5. b
Vocabulary Reinforcement: A) 1. a; 2. b; 3. b; 4. a; 5. d; 6. d; B) 1. popular; 2. around the world; 3. translated; 4. apartment; 5. earned

Language Notes

• *Popular* (Unit 1) is recycled in the definitions for *successful* and *take off*. It is also used in the main text.

• *Earn* is usually used with money or a qualification. For example: *He earned a lot of money last year. She earned her degree by studying at night.*

• *Apartment* means a rented group of rooms in which someone lives instead of living in a house. It typically includes at least one bedroom, a living or sitting room, a kitchen, and a bathroom or toilet. In places where British English is spoken, the word *flat* is more common.

• *A number of* is used when the exact number is not known or isn't important.

• *Take off* is used as an idiom in this unit to mean "become popular" but it also can mean to physically leave the ground as in: *The plane took off on time.* It might be helpful to use the image of a plane taking off because it visually expresses the idea of sudden success associated with the idiom.

Writing Extension

Have students write a fan letter to J. K. Rowling to say how they feel about the Harry Potter books. They might write about their favorite book or tell what they like about Harry himself. *Do you like the Harry Potter books or films? If so, which one do you like best? Why?*

Suggested approach:
I really like Harry Potter. I've read three of the books and seen one of the movies. So far, I like _____ best because . . .

Listening & Speaking Extension

The task is to get students to re-tell their favorite Harry Potter episode. If a student hasn't read any of the books, or seen any of the films, partner him or her with students who have.

1. First, survey the class to ensure that most students are familiar with the Harry Potter stories.

2. Tell the students that they should think of their favorite *scene* (you might have to explain this term) from Harry Potter. They will each have one minute to tell others in their group about the scene.

3. Ask students to work in small groups of four or five. Each group has a timekeeper who makes sure that the storyteller stays within the time allowed.

4. After one person tells the story, time is allowed for questions before another person has a turn. The person who just had a turn as storyteller becomes the timekeeper.

5. The activity continues until each person has had a chance to describe a scene.

Background Information

There are many Harry Potter web sites. Try http://harrypotter.warnerbros.com or http://www.bloomsburymagazine.com/harrypotter/ to learn more about the Potter books and films. See http://www.jkrowling.com/ for publishers around the world.

Unit 3 Bubble Gum

For general guidelines on how to teach a unit, see pages 5 to 8. For suggestions on ways to present and practice vocabulary and idioms, see pages 13 to 19.

Unit Summary

Target Vocabulary	Idioms
rubber, taste, chew, improve, discover, inventor	by accident (4), now and then (13), give up (18)

Answers

Target Vocabulary: 1. a; 2. f; 3. d; 4. b; 5. c; 6. e
Reading Comprehension: 1. c; 2. d; 3. a; 4. b; 5. c
Vocabulary Reinforcement: A) 1. c; 2. d; 3. b; 4. d; 5. a; 6. c; B) 1. discovered; 2. rubber; 3. now and then; 4. gave up; 5. improved

Language Notes

This unit contains two sets of potentially confusing words because the differences in meaning are subtle. Go over the differences and ask the class to come up with examples to show that they understand the meaning.

• The first set consists of three new verbs which all take place in the mouth: *bite* (from Unit 1), *taste*, and *chew*. *Bite* means to cut or tear with the teeth and requires opening the mouth. *Taste* and *chew* both occur within the closed mouth. Taste is one of the five senses and is done with the tongue. *Chew* involves breaking down food with the teeth. Check understanding of these terms by asking students to mime them. Taste can also be checked with the old experiment of giving a blindfolded student tiny amounts of sugar and salt and seeing if s/he can tell them apart—a good way to check on the idiom from Unit 1 too!

• The second set of confusing terms is *invent* and *discover*. *Invent* means to think up or create something for the first time whereas *discover* means to learn about something that already exists. You can *invent* a new machine, but you would *discover* a previously unknown star. Call out associated words and ask students to say *invent* or *discover*. For example: television, cell phones, and electric toothbrushes for *invent* and a Pacific island or an unknown type of bird for *discover*.

• The idiom *now and then* has the sense of "occasionally" so this might be a good time to review adverbs of frequency. Other adverbs of frequency you might want to review include: always, never, sometimes, occasionally, often, rarely, hardly ever. What activities do they do *now and then*?

Writing Extension

Most schools don't allow gum chewing in class. Have students write a reaction piece in their notebooks giving their opinion about whether such rules are fair or not. *Do you think rules against chewing gum are fair? Give your opinion and say why you feel this way.*

> **Suggested approach:**
> *I think that rules against chewing gum are unfair because . . .*

Listening & Speaking Extension

The task is to describe how to use bubble gum.

1. Tell the class that someone who has never chewed bubble gum will visit them. This person would like to learn how to chew gum. Students must be able to explain the steps involved in chewing gum and making big bubbles.

2. Ask students to work in small groups of four or five. Each group discusses the process and selects someone to demonstrate to the visitor. Then the class takes turn listening to the demonstrators.

Background Information

For further information on the history of chewing gum, Thomas Adams, or inventors in general, try **http://inventors.about.com/library/inventors/blgum. htm.** For information on a science project for the biggest bubble, go to **http://spidey.sfusd.k12.ca.us/ schwww/sch773/review/gumproject.html.** To learn about chewing gum around the world, visit **http://www.gumcollector.com/.**

Unit 4 The Leaning Tower

For general guidelines on how to teach a unit, see pages 5 to 8. For suggestions on ways to present and practice vocabulary and idioms, see pages 13 to 19.

Unit Summary

Target Vocabulary	Idioms
bell, lean, sink, tower, mistake, straight	as soon as (6), fall apart (19), figure out (10)

Answers

Target Vocabulary: 1. d; 2. e; 3. a; 4. b; 5. f; 6. c
Reading Comprehension: 1. b; 2. b; 3. c; 4. a; 5. c
Vocabulary Reinforcement: A) 1. b; 2. d; 3. c; 4. a; 5. d; 6. b; **B)** 1. straight; 2. leans; 3. mistake; 4. tower; 5. as soon as

Language Notes

• Three of the new vocabulary words are best explained by miming: *lean, sink,* and *straight.* Sometimes *lean* implies that part of your weight is supported by the thing you're leaning against. The word is often collocated with *against* so it's a good way to introduce this combination. *Straight* could be presented as a contrast to *bent* or *curved.*

• *As soon as* has a sense of immediacy. In fact, in British English, *immediately* could be used synonymously with *as soon as.* The phrase means directly or without delay. No time elapses between one thing and the next action. *As soon as Jane got home, the phone rang.* It happened the moment she walked in the door.

• The idiom *figure out* implies that there is a puzzle or a problem that needs to be solved. *Figure out* has a similar meaning to *work out* (introduced in Unit 14).

Writing Extension

Ask the students to brainstorm about a famous building or monument in their country. Why is this place well known? Have small groups of students design and write a travel brochure about a famous building. Here are some of the things they should include: *What is the building and where is it? What is special about this place? Why should visitors come to see it? What suggestions do you have about their visit? Give your opinion and say why you feel this way.*

Suggested approach:
You should come and visit . . . because . . .

Listening & Speaking Extension

The task is to describe a dream trip to a famous place.

1. Pretend that there is a contest for free air tickets for four people in the class to go anywhere in the world.

2. Ask students to work in small groups and discuss where they'd like to go and why. Each group will have only two minutes to make a presentation about why they should win the tickets.

Background Information

Check **http://www.pbs.org/wgbh/nova/pisa/** for a teacher's guide from a public television program on the Leaning Tower. This has a special section on rescuing world monuments including the Sphinx (Egypt), Windsor Castle (Britain), and Borobudur (Indonesia). An excellent architectural web site with 3D models of famous buildings is at **http://www.greatbuildings.com/gbc.html** and you can find UNESCO's World Heritage program at **http://whc.unesco.org/nwhc/pages/home/pages/homepage.htm.**

Unit 5 Talking Birds

For general guidelines on how to teach a unit, see pages 5 to 8. For suggestions on ways to present and practice vocabulary and idioms, see pages 13 to 19.

Unit Summary

Target Vocabulary	Idioms
brain, cage, copy, prize, nest, intelligent	stand out (12), take care of (16), turn out (20)

Answers

Target Vocabulary: 1. c; **2.** f; **3.** a; **4.** d; **5.** e; **6.** b
Reading Comprehension: 1. d; **2.** a; **3.** a; **4.** c; **5.** b
Vocabulary Reinforcement: A) 1. a; **2.** c; **3.** c; **4.** d;
5. b; **6.** a; **B) 1.** brains; **2.** copy; **3.** prize; **4.** took
care of; **5.** cage

Language Notes

• Ask students if they know some synonyms for
intelligent. They may say *bright, brilliant, clever,* or
smart. This is a good opportunity to point out that
brilliant and *smart* have additional meanings in
British English. In British English, *brilliant* is a
colloquial comment that means "excellent" and
smart often refers to physical appearance as in:
You should wear smart casual clothes to the party.
When *brilliant* refers to intelligence, it means
extremely intelligent—a genius.

• *Cage* ties in nicely with *zoo* from Unit 1. In
many places in Asia, it's popular to keep birds in
cages. Some people even take them outdoors for a
walk. Ask if people do this where your students are
from.

• *Turn out* has a similar sense as *by accident* from
Unit 3. There's a certain degree of chance in both
idioms. Explain that *turn out* is used when the
result is unexpected. *Jack was surprised when the
old letters he discovered by accident turned out to
be very valuable.*

• The idiom *take care of* has a common British
English equivalent: *to look after.* Both refer to
caring for something or someone that can't manage
by itself such as a small child or a pet.

Writing Extension

Ask the students to write about communicating
with a pet in their journals. *What kind of pet is it?
How do they communicate with the animal? Give
an example of a case where the animal understood
what people were saying. How can you tell?*

> **Suggested approach:**
> *My pet . . . understands what people say. For
> example, . . .*

Listening & Speaking Extension

Divide the class into two parts and have them
debate whether animals can "talk."

1. Team A will take the position that some
   animals, like birds and certain primates
   (monkeys and apes), can actually use language.
   Team B will argue that only people can really
   use language.

2. Ask students to talk together and come up with
   some ideas to support their position.

3. Have each team select two spokespeople to
   represent them. Everyone else becomes the
   audience.

4. Then the teams each have two chances to put
   forth their point of view. Turns are arranged A,
   B, A, B.

5. At the end, the audience votes about which
   team was most convincing.

Background Information

Check **http://www.alexfoundation.org/research/
articles/birdsusa.html** on teaching birds to talk.
For information on talking birds in the news,
history, and the arts, see **http://www.blueray.com/
wordsworth/**.

Unit 6 Valentine's Day

For general guidelines on how to teach a unit, see pages 5 to 8. For suggestions on ways to present and practice vocabulary and idioms, see pages 13 to 19.

Unit Summary

Target Vocabulary	Idioms
message, gloves, celebrate, festival, belief, underwear	all of a sudden (Did You Know?), fall in love (1), at first (4)

Answers

Target Vocabulary: 1. e; 2. d; 3. c; 4. f; 5. b; 6. a
Reading Comprehension: 1. a; 2. c; 3. b; 4. b; 5. c
Vocabulary Reinforcement: A) 1. d; 2. b; 3. d;
4. b; 5. c; 6. c; B) 1. fall in love; 2. festival;
3. celebrated; 4. gloves; 5. messages

Language Notes

• It's assumed that the students are familiar with the word *romantic*. Many will be, but it's best to check before you start the lesson since the preliminary questions use the word, as do the reading comprehension questions.

• There's potential confusion between the words *celebrate* and *festival* because they are often associated. Check that students understand that *celebrate* is a verb whereas *festival* is a noun, meaning a kind of event. It's a good time to ask about festivals that they know.

• You can connect *all of a sudden* with *at first* by eliciting time idioms used so far in the book and their synonyms. For example, *now and then* and *as soon as*. Use a diagram and sort the idioms in several ways: by something that happens all at once, something over a longer time, by where you'd use them in a sentence, etc. Try to elicit many synonyms so the students can make connections with what they already know.

Writing Extension

Ask the students to design a Valentine's message, or if this might be embarrassing for your students, another kind of card. It could be a traditional card, but it could also be something such as a Web message. Have students consider: *Who is it for? What do they want to say? What kind of message do they want (e.g., funny, romantic, serious, etc.)?*

If there's a picture, does it add to the verbal message?

Listening & Speaking Extension

Ask students to speak about festivals they know.

1. Have students work in small groups of four or five. Each group should think of a festival they know about. As soon as they have decided on a festival, write the name of that festival on the board. Other groups will have to come up with different festivals. This encourages groups to focus quickly so they get their first choice.

2. Within each group, students should share what they know about the festival: its history, when and where it is celebrated, who celebrates it, how it is celebrated, and the other things that are connected to the festival. They should prepare to act out this festival in front of the rest of the class.

3. Each team has two minutes to present their festival. First, they mime what goes on in the festival and the rest of the class tries to guess what it is. Then they briefly explain the highlights of the festival.

Background Information

For the history of the greeting card, see **http://www.emotionscards.com/museum/history. html** or **http://www.birthdays.co.uk/whatsnew/ history_main.htm**. For background information on the reading in the quiz, visit **http://news.bbc. co.uk/2/hi/uk_news/642175.stm**. This site is good for the Holi festival in India: **http://www. theholidayspot.com/holi/**. A site on holidays designed for English learners is found at **http://www.english-zone.com/holidays/symbols. html**. It features hearts, roses, and cupids.

Unit 7 The Taj Mahal

For general guidelines on how to teach a unit, see pages 5 to 8. For suggestions on ways to present and practice vocabulary and idioms, see pages 13 to 19.

Unit Summary

Target Vocabulary	Idioms
bury, cruel, marble, roof, history, beside	as for (23), find out (13), take part in (22)

Answers

Target Vocabulary: 1. f; **2.** d; **3.** e; **4.** b; **5.** a; **6.** c
Reading Comprehension: 1. c; **2.** a; **3.** b; **4.** c; **5.** c
Vocabulary Reinforcement: A) 1. c; **2.** b; **3.** d; **4.** b; **5.** a; **6.** a; **B) 1.** buried; **2.** roof; **3.** history; **4.** find out; **5.** cruel

Language Notes

• To present the word *roof* and contrast it with *ceiling*, draw a picture on the board. A roof is on the top of a building, outside, while a ceiling is inside a room.

• Note that *bury* can refer to putting anything in the ground (such as buried treasure). You can *bury* something under other things as well. *That paper was buried under all the things on my desk.*

• You can connect *find out* with *discover* from Unit 3. Both are used with an object or with a phrase starting with "that." *He found out that he was about to lose his job. She discovered that you should never touch an angry lion.*

• *As for* usually signals a contrast or a shift of topic. In the reading, there's a shift from what Shah Jahan did after building the Taj Mahal to his own burial. *Snow White married the prince and lived happily ever after. As for the dwarfs, they went back to their home in the forest.*

Writing Extension

Ask the students to write a reaction piece in which they say what kind of person Shah Jahan really was. *Was he romantic or cruel? Why do you think so?*

> **Suggested approach:**
> *In my opinion, Shah Jahan was a really romantic person because . . .*

Listening & Speaking Extension

Use categories in a class competition to help students make connections between new vocabulary. It also helps to activate prior knowledge and integrate it with recent learning.

1. Come up with about ten categories for the vocabulary words and idioms. Some examples: *buildings, animals, subjects* (e.g., *history*), *clothes, two- or three-part verbs, words to describe people,* etc.

2. Divide the class into two teams. Explain that you will alternate between teams for each category. You will give the category and ask for appropriate words. Students must listen because words can only be used once. If a word is repeated, the other team wins for that category.

3. Keep going between the two teams. When one team can't produce an acceptable word, the other team gets the point for that category. At the end, the team with the most points wins.

Background Information

Check **http://www.taj-mahal.net/** for an award-winning online virtual tour. The Taj Mahal and other famous buildings can be explored at **http://www.greatbuildings.com/buildings/ Taj_Mahal.html**. See **http://travel.guardian.co.uk/ Print/0,3858,4697495,00.html** for background information on the news item featured in the unit quiz.

Unit 8 A Winning Dream

For general guidelines on how to teach a unit, see pages 5 to 8. For suggestions on ways to present and practice vocabulary and idioms, see pages 13 to 19.

Unit Summary

Target Vocabulary	Idioms
period, lucky, bet, dream, race, win	come true (1), off and on (19), put (something) to good use (7)

Answers

Target Vocabulary: 1. d; 2. c; 3. f; 4. e; 5. b; 6. a
Reading Comprehension: 1. b; 2. c; 3. b; 4. a; 5. d
Vocabulary Reinforcement: A) 1. b; 2. c; 3. b; 4. d; 5. d; 6. a; B) 1. dreams; 2. races; 3. bet; 4. came true; 5. won

Language Notes

• Help students understand that *period* refers to a span of time, not just one point. Give examples such as a range of years (*the 1960s* meaning 1960 through 1969) and then check understanding. It is helpful to introduce vocabulary for specific *periods* of time such as a *decade* (10 years) and a *century* (100 years).

• In this unit *bet* refers to gambling money on horses. It is also used informally to refer to something that you're <u>sure</u> will happen: *I bet it's going to rain soon.*

• *Dream* can be a verb (*I often dream about flying*), a noun (*I had a bad dream*), and an adjective (*my dream house*). Have students produce examples of all three uses as a warm-up to the writing task described below.

• *Off and on* (also written as *on and off*) has much the same meaning as *now and then* from Unit 3 or the phrase *from time to time.*

Writing Extension

Students should write in their journals about a dream they have had. *What is the dream? Has it happened more than once? Could it come true? What does it mean?*

> **Suggested approach:**
> *My favorite dream is about . . . I have had this dream many times. It's possible that it could come true, but . . . I think it means . . .*

Listening & Speaking Extension

Students work in small groups and talk about types of races they know. Then they challenge other groups to think of all the information they know about a particular type of race.

1. Have the class work in small groups. They talk about types of races and make short notes about the information they know. Give some examples: *horse races, the Tour de France bicycle race, a sailboat race, a running marathon,* etc.

2. Decide randomly which group will go first. The first group asks about one kind of race. Any other team can answer as long as they can talk about that race for <u>one minute</u>. They can say where it's held, who participates, famous winners, or prizes the winner gets. When that team finishes, other teams can speak on the <u>same</u> topic, but they can't repeat any information given by the previous team. The last team to contribute information successfully for one minute gets to ask about the next kind of race.

3. The winning team of the previous round asks about a completely different race. The same rules about contributing new information and not repeating information hold. The team that participates successfully the most times wins.

Background Information

Check **http://horseracing.about.com/mbody.htm** for useful information about famous horses, races, the history of racing, and terminology. The *Life with Horses* site discusses a wide range of topics: **http://horsecity.com/lifewith/**. For details on the best-selling book and film about the famous horse Seabiscuit, see **http://www.seabiscuitonline.com/**.

Unit 9 The Mobius Band

For general guidelines on how to teach a unit, see pages 5 to 8. For suggestions on ways to present and practice vocabulary and idioms, see pages 13 to 19.

Unit Summary

Target Vocabulary	Idioms
connect, strange, surface, prove, twist, band	in other words (18), kind of (19), turn into (21)

Answers

Target Vocabulary: 1. d; **2.** b; **3.** f; **4.** a; **5.** e; **6.** c
Reading Comprehension: 1. c; **2.** b; **3.** b; **4.** a; **5.** c
Vocabulary Reinforcement: A) 1. a; **2.** c; **3.** b; **4.** d; **5.** c; **6.** a; **B) 1.** twist; **2.** band; **3.** surface; **4.** prove; **5.** strange

Language Notes

• *Surface* is best explained by demonstration. Have students identify the surfaces in your classroom and in other areas students are familiar with (e.g., desks, whiteboard, the floor, the playground). Review *rubber* and *marble* from earlier units and perhaps introduce words for other common surface materials such as *wood*, *plastic*, and *metal*.

• The idiom *in other words* is usually used for clarification, in a similar way to *i.e.* (*id est*—Latin for *that is*). This presents a good opportunity to review idioms that appear at the beginning of sentences. Idioms used as discourse markers, such as *at first* and *as for* feature in the Unit Quiz for this unit. Draw students' attention to those followed by commas.

• *Kind of* is used in several ways. As two separate words preceded by "the," it is synonymous with "the type of" or "the sort of" as in: *Maria is the kind of person who would do anything to help you.* In colloquial English, the two words are often run together and pronounced "kinda." The expression is an informal substitute for "rather" or "quite." *Lynn is kind of shy, but she likes to go to parties.*

• If you have time, there are many stories and legends that use the idea of *turn out*. For example the frog that turned out to be a prince. The fairytale tradition is rich in such stories. What examples can your students think of?

Writing Extension

Ask the students to write about a process that they know well, such as brushing teeth or leaving a message on an answering machine. Tell them that they should describe this common process as though they are giving directions to someone from a very different culture, who is totally unfamiliar with the process.

Listening & Speaking Extension

Have students work in pairs to make Mobius bands. Review the markers that are used for sequence such as *first, second, next, after that, then*, and *finally*. Note that *next, after that*, and *then* can be used in a different order.

1. Follow the reading passage step by step. This time, have them number the steps.

2. Each person explains the steps of making and marking a Mobius band as the other person listens. The listener checks the sequence and prompts the speaker if there are any problems.

3. Then the partners swap roles.

Background Information

Go to **http://www.geom.uiuc.edu/zoo/features/mobius/** for more on Mobius bands. See **http://www.cpm.informatics.bangor.ac.uk/sculpmath/pagesm/mb.html** where The Centre for the Popularisation of Mathematics shows the relationship between mathematics and the arts. It provides experiments and rotating 3D pictures of Mobius bands. Drexel University sponsors The Math Forum (**http://mathforum.org/pow/**) where Problems of the Week (PoWs) are designed to provide creative, logical challenges for elementary and high school students.

Unit 10 A Long Weekend

For general guidelines on how to teach a unit, see pages 5 to 8. For suggestions on ways to present and practice vocabulary and idioms, see pages 13 to 19.

Unit Summary

Target Vocabulary	Idioms
terrible, dangerous, tired, shout, trapped, elevator	end up (doing something) (17), get in (6), get out of (8)

Answers

Target Vocabulary: 1. c; 2. d; 3. f; 4. e; 5. a; 6. b
Reading Comprehension: 1. a; 2. b; 3. b; 4. c; 5. d
Vocabulary Reinforcement: A) 1. b; **2.** d; **3.** c; **4.** a; **5.** b; **6.** c; **B) 1.** terrible; **2.** got in; **3.** trapped; **4.** shout; **5.** ended up

Language Notes

• *Terrible* has many synonyms and antonyms, including the synonyms *horrible* or *awful* and the antonym *wonderful*. Find out which ones your class knows. Make a list of positive and negative terms and then discuss which ones you'd use in certain circumstances. Use a scale on the board to show degrees of good and bad.

• Note that *lift* is more commonly used than *elevator* in British English. Are your students familiar with the English words for other ways to travel up and down within a building? *Steps* are typically outside a building while *stairs* are inside. Are the students familiar with the word *escalator*?

• You can connect *end up* with two idioms presented earlier: *by accident* and *turn out*. All are used in a situation that ends differently than originally planned. *We planned a picnic, but we ended up at the zoo. At first, we thought we'd have a picnic, but as it turned out, we ate in a restaurant.* A synonym is *finish up*.

• You could use the idioms in this unit as an opportunity to introduce idioms and other collocations containing the word *get*, including: *get on, get up, get out, get down,* and so on. Many of these are covered in later units in the *Reading Advantage* series.

Writing Extension

Ask the students to write about what they would do if they were trapped in an elevator. *How would*

you manage? What do you usually have with you that you could use to get help? How would you feel? What would you do if your cell phone didn't work?

> **Suggested approach:**
> *If I were trapped in an elevator, I'd use my cell phone to call . . . If that didn't work, I'd . . .*

Listening & Speaking Extension

The students will work in groups of five to seven students and tell stories using positive and negative vocabulary.

1. Divide the class into small groups. Ask each group to form a circle.

2. Within the circle, one person starts to tell a story about a stressful or exciting experience. The lead person provides one sentence that must contain a positive (terrific) or negative (terrible) word.

3. The next person in the circle must repeat the first sentence and expand the story by adding a line, again using a descriptive adjective.

4. The story goes around the circle until everyone has had a turn and an ending has been developed.

5. If there is time, groups can tell their story to other groups.

Background Information

In a number of countries, including France and Japan, there has been a movement to shorten the traditional forty-hour work week to thirty-five or even thirty hours. Supporters believe that by working shorter hours and having the weekend free, workers will have a lot less stress. They also think that a shorter work week will allow workers to spend more time with their families. An additional benefit would be that a shorter work week should provide employment for a greater number of people. See **http://lamar.colostate.edu/ ~terrel/** for coverage of these topics. The site has excellent links to the issues involved.

Unit 11 Michelle Yeoh

For general guidelines on how to teach a unit, see pages 5 to 8. For suggestions on ways to present and practice vocabulary and idioms, see pages 13 to 19.

Unit Summary

Target Vocabulary	Idioms
cop, huge, prepare, role, scene, train	quite a few (2), work out (12), star in (16)

Answers

Target Vocabulary: 1. b; **2.** f; **3.** c; **4.** a; **5.** d; **6.** e
Reading Comprehension: 1. a; **2.** a; **3.** b; **4.** c; **5.** d
Vocabulary Reinforcement: A) 1. c; **2.** b; **3.** a; **4.** b; **5.** d; **6.** a; **B) 1.** starred in; **2.** role; **3.** train; **4.** prepare; **5.** scenes

Language Notes

• *Work out* in this unit (to exercise) has a completely different meaning from *work out* in Unit 14, "to finish or solve in a good way." *Work out* can also mean "find the answer to."

• *Cop* is only used informally, usually in spoken English; in more formal situations, *police officer* is better.

• *Train* and *prepare* may seem similar in meaning, but *prepare* means to make the necessary arrangements before an event, whereas *training* refers to the physical exercises that someone does to get ready for a sporting event.

• Other vocabulary you may wish to pre-teach to your students: *grow up, worldwide* (around the world).

• Female actors are also known as *actresses*.

Writing Extension

Have students make a journal entry. They should answer the following questions: *Who are your favorite actors (actresses)? Why do you like them? What do you know about them? What films have they been in? What is your favorite film? Why?*

Suggested approach:
One actor I really like is . . . I like him (her) because . . . He (she) has starred in . . . I also like . . . My favorite film is . . . because . . .

Listening & Speaking Extension

Have students play a game of twenty questions (see page 15). Demonstrate for the class first.

1. Choose a famous movie star, and have the class ask you yes/no questions to guess who the person is. Sample questions: *Are you American? Are you a man? Are you alive? Were you born in Hong Kong? Have you been in any / Do you star in (action films, sci-fi movies, etc.)?*

2. Elicit some other questions from the class, and write them on the board.

3. After the class guesses who you are thinking of, divide them into groups and have them play the game within their groups.

Background Information

Michelle Yeoh (1962–) made her film debut in the Hong Kong film *The Owl vs. Dumbo* (*Mao tou ying yu xiao fei xiang*) in 1984. **Bruce Lee** (1940–1973) was a Hong Kong-born American martial arts star. He spoke English, Cantonese, Mandarin, and Japanese. **Jackie Chan** (1954–) is famous for doing all his own stunts in his films— leaving him with many broken bones. **Chow Yun Fat** (1955–), like Jackie Chan, has moved from Asian action films to large budget Hollywood blockbusters. **Angela Mao** (1950–), a trained martial artist, starred with Bruce Lee in *Enter the Dragon* (1973). She retired from film in 1982 to spend time with her family.

For more information on Michelle Yeoh, see **www.michelleyeoh.info.** Other sites for movie information are: the Internet Movie Database (**www.imdb.com**), the Asian Movie Database (**www.asiandb.com**), Rotten Tomatoes (**www.rottentomatoes.com**), and All Movie Guide (**www.allmovie.com**).

Unit 12 Studying Abroad

For general guidelines on how to teach a unit, see pages 5 to 8. For suggestions on ways to present and practice vocabulary and idioms, see pages 13 to 19.

Unit Summary

Target Vocabulary	Idioms
require, fee, form, apply, graduate, enter	no matter (6), fill out (24), save time/money (23)

Answers

Target Vocabulary: 1. f; **2.** d; **3.** a; **4.** c; **5.** b; **6.** e
Reading Comprehension: 1. c; **2.** b; **3.** d; **4.** d; **5.** a
Vocabulary Reinforcement: A) 1. c; **2.** b; **3.** b; **4.** a;
5. c; **6.** d; **B) 1.** no matter; **2.** graduate; **3.** forms;
4. fee; **5.** enter

Language Notes

• Ensure that your class understands that the term *abroad* means a foreign or different country. Do they know students who have gone abroad to study?

• The target vocabulary in this unit presents a good opportunity to introduce suffixes. Write the words *requirement, application, graduation,* and *entrance* on the board and ask students how these words are different in meaning. Then write *improve* (improvement), *publish* (publication), *celebrate* (celebration), *prepare* (preparation), *connect* (connection), and *translate* (translation) from earlier units and have the students transform them into the noun forms in parentheses.

• Sometimes students confuse *fee* with *free*. Point out that the "r" makes a big difference!

• *Graduate* implies more than just finishing school. It normally means that you earn a qualification such as a degree, diploma, or certificate. Ask what qualification your students will earn when they graduate.

• *Save time/money* can be extended to saving energy or anything else that is valuable.
Form can also mean "the shape or structure of something," or "a kind or type of something."

Writing Extension

Tell the students that they will write a letter to a friend (real or imaginary) who is studying abroad. The purpose of the letter is to ask questions about what they would need to do to study in the same place. *Where is the place? What kind of a course or program is it? What do you have to do to get into it? What do you have to do before you go and what do you do in the other country?*

> **Suggested approach:**
> *I'm writing to ask some questions about your studies in . . . Could you please tell me about your program and what you had to do to get into it?*

Listening & Speaking Extension

1. The students will work in groups of five to seven and come up with strategies for preparing to study abroad.

2. Divide the class into small groups. You provide each group with the name of an English-speaking country such as the United States, Britain, Australia, Canada, New Zealand, etc. Each group has a different country.

3. Within each group, students discuss what they need to do to study in that country. In particular, what do they know about entrance requirements and examinations.

4. After about five minutes, each group chooses a representative who will present to the entire class.

Background Information

There are many excellent Internet sites for students interested in studying abroad. A good general site that provides links to many others is Dave's ESL Cafe at **http://www.eslcafe.com/search/**.
The major examination boards also provide information. For TOEFL, see **http://www.toefl.org/** and for IELTS go to **http://www.ielts.org**.

For general guidelines on how to teach a unit, see pages 5 to 8. For suggestions on ways to present and practice vocabulary and idioms, see pages 13 to 19.

Unit Summary

Target Vocabulary	Idioms
palace, cave, desert, furniture, block, disappear	show the way (14), over time (7), made out of (2)

Answers

Target Vocabulary: 1. f; 2. e; 3. d; 4. a; 5. c; 6. b
Reading Comprehension: 1. d; 2. c; 3. b; 4. c; 5. a
Vocabulary Reinforcement: A) 1. b; 2. b; 3. d; 4. a; 5. c; 6. c; B) 1. unique; 2. desert; 3. made out of; 4. blocks; 5. Palace

Language Notes

• In the Before You Read section, point out the word *memorable* and elicit its meaning. Can the students see another word they know within this word? (*memory, remember*) This is a good technique for guessing the meaning of new words in context.

• This unit provides a good opportunity to discuss *deserts* around the world. Students are probably familiar with the Sahara and the Gobi, but may not know others. An extension activity might involve having students use maps or atlases to identify other deserts.

• Two useful words appear in this unit that are not part of the target vocabulary list: *unique* and *guide*. Point out that *unique* means "one of a kind" and therefore cannot be used with a modifier such as *very*. *Guide* can be a person (noun), a verb, or a noun modifier (*guide* dogs for the blind).

• *Show the way* implies that someone is lost or unfamiliar with an area. *Can you show me the way* is a useful expression for students who are studying abroad and need to ask for help.

• *Made of* can be used to mean *made out of*.

• The prefix *dis-* used in *disappear* is a common one, meaning *not*. Other examples include *disadvantage, disallow, disapprove*. Can your students come up with any others?

Writing Extension

This writing extension is a group exercise. Divide the class into groups of four. Each group is going to create a Dream Hotel and produce a brochure about its main features. If possible, show some travel brochures to students before they start so they can see what is expected. Here are some things to consider: *Where is it? What's it like? Is it special or unique in some way? What can people do there? How do they travel there? Are guides available?*

Suggested approach:
For the holiday of a lifetime, stay at . . . Since it's in the middle of the desert, you arrive by . . . It's twenty kilometers from the nearest town . . .

Listening & Speaking Extension

This listening/speaking activity is an extension of the writing activity in this unit.

1. Have students in each group prepare a spoken presentation for the hotel they have prepared a brochure for.

2. Each group will appoint a speaker (or speakers) who will present their hotel to the class.

3. The class listens to each presentation, then votes on which hotel sounds most attractive.

Background Information

A Web search of the keywords "salt palace hotel" should turn up a selection of sites offering tours to the Salt Palace Hotel, including color photographs. See **www.palmisland.co.ae** for a virtual tour of the Palm Islands project described in the Quiz. To find other exotic holiday destinations, search a search engine, such as Yahoo (**http://travel.yahoo.com/**) or Google Directory (**http://directory.google.com/Top/Recreation/Travel/**), under the travel category.

Unit 14 Trying Again

For general guidelines on how to teach a unit, see pages 5 to 8. For suggestions on ways to present and practice vocabulary and idioms, see pages 13 to 19.

Unit Summary

Target Vocabulary	Idioms
couple, (to) date, divorce, marriage, match, program	work out (2), break up (with someone) (4), (be) made for each other (15)

Answers

Target Vocabulary: 1. c; **2.** d; **3.** f; **4.** b; **5.** e; **6.** a
Reading Comprehension: 1. d; **2.** b; **3.** b; **4.** a; **5.** b
Vocabulary Reinforcement: A) 1. b; **2.** d; **3.** d; **4.** c; **5.** a; **6.** a; **B) 1.** working out; **2.** divorce; **3.** dating; **4.** match; **5.** couple

Language Notes

• Start a discussion about marriage patterns in your country. *Who can you marry and who decides who you marry? Are most marriages successful? What happens if a marriage doesn't work out?*

• You may want to draw attention to the word *legal*, which appears in the definitions for marriage and divorce. Note that *legal* can refer to either government or religious law, depending on the place it is used.

• *Work out* is used differently in this unit than in Unit 11 where it relates to exercise. The meaning here is closer to *turn out* from Unit 5—*to end up.*

• *Break up* is an informal way of saying that a relationship has *fallen apart* (Unit 4). A more formal way of saying this is *separate.*

• *Match* also has various meanings as a noun: "a football game," and "something used to light fires."

• *Couple* is not only used to refer to people. It can be used to refer to two or three of anything: "a couple of minutes," "a couple of sandwiches," etc.

• *Program* is spelled *programme* in British English.

Writing Extension

Students will write their opinions on the concept of being "made for each other." Do a couple have to match to have a successful marriage? Encourage students to support their opinions with examples.

Suggested approach:
I disagree that a couple has to be "made for each other" in order to have a good marriage. In my country, . . .

Listening & Speaking Extension

The students will work in small groups to discuss what makes a relationship successful.

1. First, they should make a list of things that contribute to relationships that work out.

2. Next, students think of unsuccessful relationships and list reasons why they think the relationship fell apart.

3. When groups are ready, have them compare their lists with the rest of the class. Have them note areas where there is agreement about the important factors.

Background Information

For such a broad topic as marriage, you might want to take several approaches. For an overview of different marriage patterns worldwide, see **http://vax.wcsu.edu/socialsci/socres.html**. In many countries people advertise in newspapers for mates. If you feel it is appropriate in your setting, it might be interesting to bring in such ads from an English language newspaper, and have students discuss which people they would be interested in, and why.

34

Unit 15 The Mona Lisa

For general guidelines on how to teach a unit, see pages 5 to 8. For suggestions on ways to present and practice vocabulary and idioms, see pages 13 to 19.

Unit Summary

Target Vocabulary	Idioms
portrait, museum, visitor, hide, steal, valuable	said to be (6), go well (5), of all time (2)

Answers

Target Vocabulary: 1. b; 2. d; 3. f; 4. c; 5. a; 6. e
Reading Comprehension: 1. d; 2. b; 3. b; 4. c; 5. c
Vocabulary Reinforcement: A) 1. c; 2. d; 3. a; 4. b; 5. c; 6. a; B) 1. said to be; 2. of all time; 3. visitors; 4. stolen; 5. hidden

Language Notes

• Museums do not only contain art, such as paintings, but can also contain things such as ancient objects from archaeological excavations, traditional objects used in daily life, and collections of certain kinds of objects.

• In the target vocabulary for Unit 15 are two verbs with irregular past forms: *hide* and *steal*. This presents a natural opportunity to go back through the vocabulary given thus far and identify other irregular verbs. You might want to divide the class into teams and see which team can accurately identify the most irregular verbs, including those in the idioms.

• The idiom *said to be* implies a certain degree of uncertainty, not fact. It often refers to general public opinion. *Mumtaz Mahal was said to be Shah Jahan's favorite wife.*

• You could point out to students that the suffix *-er* (or *-or*) from *visitor* refers to "one who does something."

• Review other idioms involving the word *go*, such as *go without, go badly*.

Writing Extension

For this unit, students will write a letter to a penfriend and tell about a famous work of art in their own country. It may be a painting, sculpture, or a historic monument. The letter should give some background about the work of art and tell why it is famous or important.

Suggested approach:
I'd like to tell you about some special things in the museum in my city. The most famous painting is . . . It is about . . . years old and people like it because . . .

Listening & Speaking Extension

1. Either download from the Internet and print five or six famous paintings of people or borrow a book of famous paintings from the library. Have the students work in groups to make up a story to tell about the paintings. Most students will not know the actual background of the paintings, but that doesn't matter. For this exercise, the more imaginative story, the better!

2. Divide the class into groups of four or five students. Give each group a picture of a painting.

3. The students have about five minutes to invent a story about the painting. Who is it? What happened before this painting was made? How did the artist know about this? Why was the painting made?

4. Then the groups take turns telling their story. At the end, the class votes on the best story.

Background Information

A Web search on Leonardo da Vinci will turn up many sites devoted to his life and art.
The Internet and encyclopedias are full of information about famous artists and their works. http://www.artcyclopedia.com/ is a good starting point. In addition, there have been some excellent educational television programs about art history, notably the one by Sister Wendy. See http://www.pbs.org/wgbh/sisterwendy/ for further details. The reading in the quiz is based on Tracey Chevalier's **Girl with a Pearl Earring** (Harper Collins, 1999) which is available worldwide in paperback. It is readable by intermediate students. The *Guinness Book of Records* (http://www. guinnessworldrecords.com) provides a great deal of fun practice for the idiom *of all time*.

Unit 16 Breakfast in America

For general guidelines on how to teach a unit, see pages 5 to 8. For suggestions on ways to present and practice vocabulary and idioms, see pages 13 to 19.

Unit Summary

Target Vocabulary	Idioms
actually, war, serve, traditional, ancient, recipe	on the go (19), long ago (12), come up with (14)

Answers

Target Vocabulary: 1. b; **2.** d; **3.** c; **4.** f; **5.** a; **6.** e
Reading Comprehension: 1. d; **2.** a; **3.** a; **4.** c; **5.** a
Vocabulary Reinforcement: A) 1. b; **2.** a; **3.** d; **4.** b; **5.** c; **6.** d; **B) 1.** actually; **2.** long ago; **3.** ancient; **4.** came up with; **5.** on the go

Language Notes

• Discuss types and names of meals as these differ from country to country. In America, *dinner* usually refers to the evening meal, but in some places the biggest meal of the week is *Sunday dinner* which is held at midday. In England, *tea* is both a meal and a drink.

• *Traditional* and *ancient* present a good opportunity to check on their opposites: *modern* and *recent*. *Ancient* is reserved for very old things, whereas *long ago* refers to the past when exact dates are either not known or are not important to the context.

• The idioms *on the go* and *come up with* are informal expressions meaning *busy* and *invent*.

• Help students understand historical sequence by using a timeline to show the relationship between events in the reading.

• *Serve* has an alternative meaning in tennis, meaning to hit the ball to start play.

Writing Extension

Students should keep a breakfast log for a week. In their notebooks, each student notes what she/he ate for breakfast, when, where, and why. Before students hand in their logs, they should look through them and write a summary of the patterns they see there.

Suggested approach:
When I looked at my breakfast log, I realized that I usually eat the most for breakfast on . . . During the week, I was on the go all the time and only had coffee and . . .

Listening & Speaking Extension

Take advantage of the introduction of more time vocabulary and idioms to give students a chance to discuss differences between how something was done long ago and how it's done now. You or the class can choose the topics, but food and exercise are good ones to start with.

1. Divide the class into three groups, A, B, and C.

2. In the first round, group A gets to say everything they can think of about how something was done <u>in the past</u> (good past tense practice!). Group B tells how it is done <u>now</u>. Group C compares the two for differences and similarities. Brainstorm discourse markers such as: *by contrast, on the other hand, however, actually*, etc.

3. After the class has gone through one topic (snack food, for example), rotate groups and discuss another topic (e.g., physical fitness). This time Group B gets to talk about the past, Group C deals with the present, and Group A compares the two.

4. If you have time, move on to a third topic, rotating the group assignments.

Background Information

There is a common saying, "Eat breakfast like a king, lunch like a prince, and dinner like a pauper." Is there an equivalent in your students' countries?

A good source for recipes for breakfast foods is **http://brunchrecipe.com/**. For those students interested in making their own breakfast cereals, **http://www.freerecipe.org/Breakfast/Cereals/** is a good starting point. **http://www.nal.usda.gov/fnic/Fpyr/pyramid.html** provides information on the food pyramid (a guideline to what kinds of foods are necessary for a healthy diet).

Unit 17 The World Cup

For general guidelines on how to teach a unit, see pages 5 to 8. For suggestions on ways to present and practice vocabulary and idioms, see pages 13 to 19.

Unit Summary

Target Vocabulary	Idioms
beat, final, match, record, score, tournament	turn attention to (1), make it to (19), come up against (6)

Answers

Target Vocabulary: 1. d; 2. c; 3. a; 4. e; 5. f; 6. b
Reading Comprehension: 1. d; 2. b; 3. d; 4. c; 5. c
Vocabulary Reinforcement: A) 1. a; 2. b; 3. d; 4. d; 5. c; 6. a; B) 1. beaten; 2. match; 3. tournament; 4. made it to; 5. scored

Language Notes

• *Final* can easily be extended to *finally*. It's a good chance to review the other time markers, e.g., *first, then, next*, and so on. Explain that they are typically used at the beginning of sentences (and therefore capitalized) and followed by a comma. They mark transitions between major points so *finally* should signal the last major point. *Finally, the tie score was broken by a sensational goal by the home team.*

• Note the distinction between *match*, which refers to a single game, and *tournament* or *competition*, a series of games.

• In the definition of *turn attention to*, ensure that students understand *focus*. You might want to use an analogy with a camera's focus.

• *Come up against* is used informally. Contrast *come up against* with *come up with* (Unit 16). Mention some other three-part verbs and have students guess the meanings. Examples include *look down on* and *get away with*.

• Explain the differences between *million* (a thousand thousand), *billion* (a thousand million), and *trillion* (a million million).

• Elicit other sports-related vocabulary from your students, e.g., *lose to, win, defeat, kick off, victory*, and so on.

Writing Extension

Have students work in small groups to design posters for their favorite sports teams. *What is the most important thing about the team? What are their colors? Do they have a mascot (a team symbol or pet)? Who are the most important players?* Display the posters on the walls.

Listening & Speaking Extension

Build on the writing task by playing twenty questions (see page 15). Each team has a turn as the focal group.

1. Just before their turn, the team can choose to be any sports personality. They don't necessarily have to choose someone from the team they previously designed posters for.

2. The other class members ask yes/no questions. *Did he play for Manchester United? Was his wife in a band?*

3. If the correct individual is guessed within twenty questions, another team comes on. If after twenty questions the identity of the sports personality is still not clear, the team gets another turn with a different personality.

Background Information

Some soccer web sites: Ronaldo (**http://www. r9ronaldo.com/eng/**), FIFA, the world soccer association (**http://www.fifa.org**). The official World Cup web site is **http://fifaworldcup. yahoo.com**. Students interested in the English Premier League should visit **http://www. premierleague.com**. The Union of European Football Associations' web site is **http://www. uefa.com/**.

Unit 18 Blood Types

For general guidelines on how to teach a unit, see pages 5 to 8. For suggestions on ways to present and practice vocabulary and idioms, see pages 13 to 19.

Unit Summary

Target Vocabulary	Idioms
attempt, curious, outgoing, generous, honest, original	be a hit (22), lose weight (22), carry out (something) (10)

Answers

Target Vocabulary: 1. e; **2.** a; **3.** c; **4.** f; **5.** b; **6.** d
Reading Comprehension: 1. b; **2.** d; **3.** d; **4.** d; **5.** a
Vocabulary Reinforcement: A) 1. a; **2.** d; **3.** c; **4.** a; **5.** b; **6.** c; **B) 1.** attempts; **2.** carried out; **3.** curious; **4.** original; **5.** been a hit

Language Notes

• *Curious, outgoing, generous, honest* and *original* are all adjectives that apply to people. Ask students to find other adjectives from the target vocabulary of previous units. They should come up with *successful* (2), *intelligent* (5), *cruel* (7), *lucky* (8), *strange* (9), *terrible, dangerous,* and *tired* (all Unit 11). Ask the class to sort words by positive and negative connotations.

• Use *be a hit* to review *take off, blockbuster, successful,* and *popular* from previous units.

• When introducing *lose weight,* discuss some of the other words used for overweight and underweight people. Which are colloquial and which are more formal? Which are polite and which are rude? Polite examples include *heavy* and *slim.* Impolite examples include *fat* and *skinny.*

• Ask what else students can lose. Examples include: *objects, one's temper, one's mind, one's way.*

• In the context of this unit, *carry out* is collocated with research project. Note that it is quite different from the literal meaning. Compare *Joe's carrying out the garbage* with *Joe's carrying out cancer research.* You can also *carry out* a procedure.

Writing Extension

Ask students to make a journal entry about their blood type, and what they think it means for their personality.

Suggested approach:
My blood is type . . . According to the passage, this means that I am . . . I agree/disagree with this. I think . . .

Listening & Speaking Extension

Divide the class into two teams and have a debate on what causes personality traits. One side will take the position that personality is inborn, determined by genetic factors such as blood type. The opposite side will argue that environment and experiences (such as upbringing and culture) are much more important.

1. Select one person to be a moderator who will keep time and order.

2. Each team gets to participate in a general discussion for about five minutes. During this time, they make notes of the most important points and choose two people to represent the rest of the team.

3. Toss a coin to decide which side goes first. Each team gets two rounds. At the end, the rest of the class decides which team had the stronger argument.

Background Information

For more information about blood types, transfusions, and giving blood, see http://www.blood.co.uk/ or the American Red Cross: http://www.redcross.org/donate/give/. For more information on the (alleged) connection between blood type and personality, do an Internet search for "blood types and personality."

Unit 19 Television

For general guidelines on how to teach a unit, see pages 5 to 8. For suggestions on ways to present and practice vocabulary and idioms, see pages 13 to 19.

Unit Summary

Target Vocabulary	Idioms
broadcast, public, concerned, murder, allow, effect	take place (1), by the time (16), get (someone) to do (something) (19)

Answers

Target Vocabulary: 1. b; **2.** e; **3.** a; **4.** f; **5.** d; **6.** c
Reading Comprehension: 1. c; **2.** d; **3.** b; **4.** c; **5.** c
Vocabulary Reinforcement: A) 1. d; **2.** b; **3.** b; **4.** c;
5. a; **6.** d; **B) 1.** broadcast; **2.** took place;
3. concerned; **4.** effects; **5.** allow

Language Notes

• *Broadcast* can be a verb or a noun. *Show* can be a noun (a TV show) or a verb (show a program).

• Contrast the meaning of *program* in this unit to the meaning of *program* for computers in Unit 14.

• Contrast *public* (which often means open to people in general) with *private* (only open to certain, special people). *This is a public beach so anyone can swim here. However, that beach is private and only open to people who live there.*

• The word most often associated with *effect* is *cause*. A *cause* is something that creates a situation and an *effect* is the result. *Watching violent cartoons on TV makes children behave badly.* Watching cartoons is the *cause*, the bad behavior is the *effect*.

• *Occur* is another synonym for *take place* or *happen*. The three can be used interchangeably.

• Note that there are three phrasal verbs in this unit that use the word *take*: *take off, take place, take part in* (from the What Do You Think? section). Ask students if they can think of any other *take* verbs.

• Use *by the time* as an opportunity to review other time-related idioms, such as those from Units 12, 13, and 15.

Writing Extension

Ask students to keep a log of television use during the next week. They should note every time they are in a room with a TV that is on, whether they are actively watching or not. They should note the length of time, the names and types of programs, and whether they watch alone or with other people. At the end of the week, they should look through their log and write a summary.

Suggested approach:
I was surprised to find that I watched TV for . . . hours last week, . . . more/less than I spent in class! I watched a mix of programs but most of the hours were spent watching . . .

Listening & Speaking Extension

1. Divide the class into groups of four or five students. Have them choose their favorite TV program and prepare a brief skit or play from it.

2. As each group performs the skit, the others try to guess what program it is. List the programs on the board.

3. When all have finished, discuss what's good and bad about each program.

Background Information

There's a large amount of literature on the effect of TV violence on children and even on adult behavior. See **http://www.apa.org/pubinfo/violence.html** for one study. TV-Turnoff Network's web site is **http://www.tvturnoff.org**.

Unit 20 Rodeos

For general guidelines on how to teach a unit, see pages 5 to 8. For suggestions on ways to present and practice vocabulary and idioms, see pages 13 to 19.

Unit Summary

Target Vocabulary	Idioms
cowboy, saddle, competition, wrestle, tie, event	all year round (15), show off (8), all over (19)

Answers

Target Vocabulary: 1. c; 2. d; 3. e; 4. f; 5. b; 6. a
Reading Comprehension: 1. d; 2. b; 3. b; 4. c; 5. d
Vocabulary Reinforcement: A) 1. b; 2. a; 3. c; 4. b; 5. d; 6. a; **B)** 1. came together; 2. cowboys; 3. showed off; 4. events; 5. wrestling

Language Notes

• Point out that *competition* is a general term. All kinds of athletic games, matches, and tournaments come under this category. Review the word *tournament*, and other vocabulary from Unit 17.

• *Wrestle* also refers to two men fighting each other without weapons such as sumo wrestling in Japan.

• *Wrestle* has a silent "w" and starts with an "r" sound. See if students can think of other words with this spelling, e.g., *write, wrong, wrinkle, wrench, wreck.*

• You can recycle *connect* in association with *tie.* The place where two ropes or strings are connected is called a *knot.*

• *Events* happen or *take place* (Unit 19) on a schedule. Some of them occur *all year round.*

• *Show off* can have a negative connotation when someone displays skills or belongings too much. Then the person can be called a "show off." *Sandy drives dangerously. He's a real show off.*

• In Reading Comprehension, question 1, make certain that students understand *origin* as a place where something started or came from. *Origin* is the root of the word *original.*

• Elicit idioms containing the word *all (all year round)*, such as *all the time,* and *all of a sudden.*

• A *calf* is a baby *cow,* and a *bull* is a male *cow.* What other words can students come up with for male, female, and baby animals?

Writing Extension

Follow on from the What Do You Think questions and have students write their opinion about whether rodeos or other animal shows are cruel. Ask them to support their opinions.

> **Suggested approach:**
> *I think it's cruel/OK to wrestle bulls in rodeos because . . .*

Listening & Speaking Extension

1. As a review for this last unit in the book, divide the students into small groups and have each group create word maps (see page 41) for related words about competitions.

2. Competitions will appear in the center of the map and other competitions mentioned in the book will radiate out. Some examples are animal shows (which would have rodeos, horse races, and bird shows as subsets), sports competitions, and beauty contests. The specific vocabulary for each one is listed with it.

3. After each map is finished, have a spokesperson from each group explain the map to the class.

Background Information

There are several good Internet sites on rodeos, including **http://www.prorodeo.com,** the women's professional rodeo association site **http://www.wpra.com/,** and the web sites for two of the organizations mentioned in the passage: **http://www.rodeojapan.com/e/index.htm** and **http://www.nonprofitpages.com/kaca/.**

Review: Units 1–5

Answers

A. 1. rubber; **2.** earn; **3.** brain; **4.** prize; **5.** popular; **6.** sink; **7.** bell; **8.** discover; **9.** afford; **10.** female
B. 1. Inventor; **2.** stands out; **3.** figuring out; **4.** improving; **5.** successful; **6.** apartment; **7.** take off; **8.** now and then; **9.** without question
C. 1. f; **2.** d; **3.** e; **4.** b; **5.** a; **6.** g
D. Across: 1. cage; **6.** published; **8.** translated; **Down: 2.** give up; **3.** collar; **4.** bite; **5.** as soon as; **6.** nest

Extension Activity: Word Maps

A **word map** is a diagram used to show the relationships between a word or idea and other related words or ideas. Word maps are a great way for students to review and reinforce vocabulary related to a topic. In this review unit, your students will practice making a word map. The best way to explain how to do this is by drawing one on the board. The main topic or idea is written in a box or circle in the middle of a blank piece of paper, and related words radiate outwards from the center. Look at the example word map, on the key word of *animals*.

As you draw lines, your map will start to look like a spider's web. You can also draw some lines darker and thicker than others to show that some connections between words are more important than others. Different sizes of box or circle can be used to show categories and subcategories. For example, in the word map below the *animals* box is largest, then the main subcategories are next largest (*air, land, water, working animals, pets, wild, etc.*). For the individual animals, such as *horse, elephant*, and so on, no box is needed. Copy the example *animals* map below onto the board, but rather than copy the words from the page, elicit them from the class.

Have students work in small groups to complete word maps. Some suggested topics are: *books, Harry Potter, food, buildings,* etc. Alternatively, elicit starting topics from the class. There are no "right answers" for word maps or webs. After groups have made one, have them compare theirs with another group, and add any interesting words they learn to their own map.

If any interesting new words arise, write them on the board, and possibly add them to the Vocabulary Box (page 15).

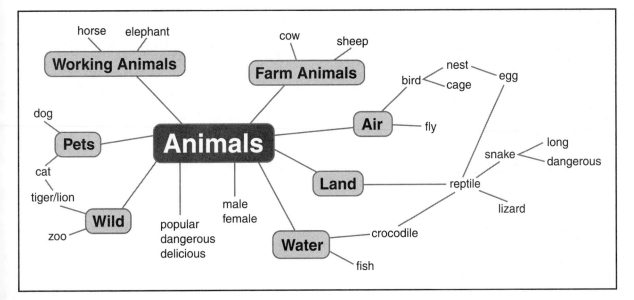

Review: Units 6–10

Answers

A. 1. underwear; **2.** connect; **3.** prove; **4.** trapped; **5.** shout; **6.** strange; **7.** message; **8.** beside; **9.** cruel; **10.** twist

B. 1. At first; **2.** take part in; **3.** end up; **4.** found out; **5.** celebrate; **6.** gloves; **7.** put them to good use; **8.** lucky

C. 1. f; **2.** a; **3.** b; **4.** c; **5.** d; **6.** g

D. Across: 1. tired; **4.** get in; **6.** roof; **7.** period; **8.** band; **10.** festival; **11.** marble; **Down: 1.** terrible; **2.** bet; **3.** kind of; **5.** elevator; **9.** dream

Extension Activity: Student-designed Tests

Students can learn a lot by making up their own review tests and giving them to other students. Here's a quick and easy way to review the new vocabulary and idioms from Units 6 through 10. Students will need to close their textbooks for this activity.

1. Before the class, make two photocopies each of the reading passages in Units 6–10.

2. Divide the class into five groups and give each group two copies of one of the readings from Units 6–10. One copy is for the group to make notes on, and the other copy will become the finished "test" that they will show to other students.

3. Have each group choose ten words or idioms from the reading that they want to test, and circle them or mark them with a highlighter. It's up to the group whether to test the whole idiom or just part of it. Sometimes it's better to only leave out one of the words so that their classmates have to pay attention to the other words near the gap or space.

4. Now change to the unmarked paper. After each group has decided which words to leave out, they need to prepare the test on the other piece of paper by hiding the words they have chosen to test. There are two ways this can be done. If correction fluid (white out, Tipex®, Liquid Paper®) is available they can use that. Alternatively, they can use a dark marker or pen and completely cover the word(s).

5. Number each of the spaces from 1 to 10.

6. Now have each group pass their test to another group. Ask them each to write the numbers 1 to 10 on a piece of paper. Then see if they can write the missing words next to the numbers. Go over the tests with them and point out any problems. Of course, students' books should be closed throughout this entire activity.

7. When a group has finished their test, have them check their answers with the group that prepared the test.

8. Continue by having the tests pass to another group until all groups have taken all the tests. By the time you finish, the class will have reviewed all the vocabulary.

Review: Units 11–15

Answers

A. 1. bury; 2. furniture; 3. visitor; 4. hide; 5. divorce; 6. valuable; 7. portrait; 8. disappear; 9. program; 10. surface

B. 1. made for each other; 2. dating; 3. graduated; 4. couple; 5. get married; 6. over time; 7. working out; 8. divorce

C. 1. d; 2. c; 3. a; 4. e; 5. g; 6. b

D. **Across:** 2. stole; 3. enter; 4. cop; 8. require; 9. palace; 11. form; 12. museum; **Down:** 1. fee; 2. scene; 5. prepare; 6. huge; 7. apply; 8. role; 10. cave

Extension Activity: Writing and Acting Dialogues

A good way to review material is to do something different with it. The main focus of the *Reading Advantage* series is reading, but this activity requires students to write a dialogue and then act it out for the rest of the class.

1. Divide the class into five groups and assign each group one of the Units 11 to 15.

2. Explain to students that they are going to write a script involving at least two people (but more if they like). Students may use the topic or theme of their unit, but they don't have to. Encourage them to use their imaginations. However, their script must include all the target vocabulary items, including the idioms from their assigned unit.

3. The first thing students must decide is who the two people are going to be. Then, where will the conversation take place? What background does the audience need so they can make sense of the conversation? What will the personalities of their characters be like?

4. When each group has written out a script, have them try with several different people reading the parts. Have each group decide who will perform each role before the rest of the class.

5. Have groups take turns presenting their dialogues. Make sure each group describes the setting or context before they start.

6. After each dialogue, encourage other members of the class to ask the actors questions.

Review: Units 16–20

Answers

A. 1. ancient; **2.** cowboy; **3.** attempt; **4.** public; **5.** curious; **6.** effect; **7.** outgoing; **8.** murder; **9.** allow; **10.** original

B. 1. all over; **2.** matches; **3.** broadcast; **4.** all year round; **5.** scores; **6.** tournament; **7.** takes place; **8.** final

C. 1. c; **2.** g; **3.** d; **4.** a; **5.** f; **6.** b

D. Across: 1. generous; **4.** made it to; **6.** war; **8.** on the go; **10.** serve; **11.** saddle; **12.** beat; **Down: 2.** event; **3.** show off; **5.** tie; **7.** recipe; **9.** honest

Extension Activity: Defining and Guessing in Pairs

This activity requires students to work in pairs and supply definitions of words to their partners.

1. Before class, label ten pieces of paper: 16A, 16B, 17A, and so on, up to 20B. On each piece of paper write three target vocabulary items and two idioms from that unit, making sure that A and B for each unit contain different items. (Since each unit presents nine new items, add an idiom to the list from Units 1–15.) Each list should have five items. Make enough copies of your lists for everyone in the class to have one list.

2. Divide students into pairs and give each pair the A and B lists for a single unit. Don't let students see their partner's list. Students will take turns defining words from their list to their partner.

3. Student A will begin by giving a definition of the first word on his/her list. The word on the list cannot be used in the definition, but they can use synonyms, antonyms, or examples. Student B will try to guess the item.

4. When Student B guesses A's first word, then s/he takes a turn defining the first word on her/his list. The same rules apply.

5. Pairs take turns going through the list until they have used all the vocabulary items. Note any words that students had problems defining or guessing. Write these words on the board.

6. Pairs should then find another pair who has finished and swap lists with them and start again. The activity should continue until all pairs have done five different lists.

7. Go through any difficult vocabulary on the board.

Introduction to Unit Quizzes

There are twenty unit quizzes—one for each of the units. Each quiz is divided into two sections, each consisting of five questions, for a total mark out of ten. The format varies from unit to unit, but following are the kinds of activities found in the quizzes.

Part 1

Match the words and definitions

Five definitions and six vocabulary items are provided, and students need to match the correct vocabulary item with each definition. To make the activity more challenging, there is always one more vocabulary item than definition.

Complete the passage

A cloze passage is provided, with five missing words and phrases. Students need to choose the appropriate word or phrase for each space from the ones provided. Again an extra item is given.

Complete the sentences

In this multiple-choice activity there are five sentences, each with a missing vocabulary item. Students must choose the appropriate item from the four options.

Find the different word

Students have to identify which one of four words is different in meaning from the others.

Find the same meaning

Similar to complete the sentences, but this time students need to identify which one of the four choices has the same meaning as the underlined portion of the sentence.

Choose the best answer

There are five questions. Students need to find the best answer for each question from the four options provided.

Part 2

Read and Answer

Students read a passage, or other material, which is thematically linked to the reading passage in the unit, and then complete an activity based on the passage. The activity may require students to . . .
- decide whether each of the five statements about the passage is true or false.
- decide whether each of the five statements about the passage is true, false, or unknown.
- answer multiple-choice questions about the passage.
- write short answers to five questions.

Organize the paragraph

Students look at several sentences and have to number them in order to make a coherent passage. To help students to get started, some of the sentences have already been numbered.

Complete the passage

This activity is the same as the complete the passage activity type in Part 1.

For more information on question types in *Reading Advantage,* see the Guide to Question Formats on pages 10 and 11. For convenience in keeping track of students' scores on the tests, as well as the unit quizzes, a photocopiable scoring sheet is provided on page 77.

Unit 1 Quiz

Name:	Score:	/10 =	%

Part 1: Match the words and definitions

Write a word or idiom from the box next to each definition below. One word or idiom is extra.

zoo	tell apart	female	collar	popular	bite

1. _____ well-liked by many people

2. _____ to cut with the teeth

3. _____ something around the neck

4. _____ a place to keep animals

5. _____ to see the difference between things

Part 2: Read and answer

Read the sign and decide if the statement is *true* or *false*. Circle your answer.

ZOO INFORMATION

LIONS

From: Lions live in the wild in Africa and India. Our lions are African lions from Kenya.

Males: We have two adult males and they weigh about 200 kilograms. They have a collar of long hair called a mane around their faces.

Females: Our zoo has four adult females. They weigh about 175 kilograms. They don't have a mane.

Young lions: Lions live in family groups called prides. Young lions are called cubs. There are six young lions in this pride. Can you tell apart the males and the females?

Feeding: We feed the lions at 9 a.m. and 4 p.m. Adult lions eat about 5 kilograms of meat a day. Zoo workers must be careful because a lion's bite is very strong!

1. true false   The lions in this zoo are from India.

2. true false   The males weigh more than the females.

3. true false   Both males and female lions have manes.

4. true false   Young lions are called "prides."

5. true false   The lions in this zoo eat twice a day.

Unit 2 Quiz

Name: _____   **Score:** _____ **/10 =** _____ **%**

▌ Part 1: Complete the passage

Use words from the box to complete the passage. Write the words in the spaces. One item is extra.

took off	translate	apartment	go without	successful	without question

My friend Laila's singing career wasn't (1)_____ at first. She was so poor she had to

(2)_____ new clothes and share a(n) (3)_____ with three other girls. Then she

had a hit song and her career (4)_____. Now, (5)_____, she's a popular star.

▌ Part 2: Read and answer

**Read about the meeting and answer the questions. Circle the letter
of the best answer.**

> ── LOVE HARRY POTTER? ──
> ♡ ♡ ♡ ♡ ♡ ♡ ♡ ♡ ♡ ♡
> ♥ Have you read all the books and seen all the movies?
> Have you read about the writer's success? ♥
> ♥ Wouldn't you like to have your book popular all
> around the world too? ♥
> ➤ If so, come to a writer's meeting at the
> library next Tuesday, July 13, at 7:30 p.m. ◀
> Learn how to get your book published and
> earn money from your writing. Come to this
> free meeting and learn the magic of success.

1. The meeting is about . . .
   - **a.** Harry Potter films.
   - **b.** popular new books.
   - **c.** how to publish.
   - **d.** travel around the world.

2. Who will go to the meeting?
   - **a.** writers
   - **b.** translators
   - **c.** children
   - **d.** librarians

3. When is the meeting?
   - **a.** this Thursday
   - **b.** next Tuesday
   - **c.** on June 13
   - **d.** at 7:30 a.m.

4. This advertisement does not say . . .
   - **a.** what time the talk is.
   - **b.** where the talk is.
   - **c.** who will give the talk.
   - **d.** why you should go to the talk.

5. The meeting . . .
   - **a.** sells Harry Potter books.
   - **b.** costs a lot.
   - **c.** shows Harry Potter films.
   - **d.** doesn't cost anything.

Unit 3 Quiz

Name:	Score:	/10 =	%

▌ Part 1: Complete the sentences

Decide which words are best for the spaces. Circle the letter of your choice.

1. You can _____ sweet or salty food with your tongue.
      a. bite   **b.** chew   **c.** blow   **d.** taste

2. There weren't any electric lights before Edison _____ them.
      a. discovered   **b.** improved   **c.** invented   **d.** earned

3. Most balloons are made from _____.
      a. gum   **b.** rubber   **c.** erasers   **d.** tires

4. Maria usually doesn't chew gum, but she does _____.
      a. very often   **b.** most days   **c.** now and then   **d.** all the time

5. Thomas didn't plan to meet his friends at the mall. They met there _____.
      a. by accident   **b.** without question   **c.** successfully   **d.** around the world

▌ Part 2: Read and answer

Read the news report and decide if the statement is *true* or *false*. Circle your answer.

Singapore, July 12 Many people enjoy chewing gum, but in 1992 Singapore decided to make it against the law. The government said that people were not careful about throwing away used gum. Instead, they dropped it on sidewalks and on the street where it made a big mess. Chewing gum also got stuck in the doors of the subway or underground trains so that the doors didn't close properly. This meant that the trains did not run on time. Singapore said that people had to give up chewing gum or pay a lot of money to the government. During the ban on chewing gum, the streets and subways of Singapore were clean.

Now the government of Singapore is changing the rules a little. Some dentists say that sugarless chewing gum can help people take care of their teeth. They have discovered that chewing gum can improve dental health. Now the government says that people will be able to buy special kinds of gum at pharmacies for health reasons. Other kinds of gum are still not allowed.

1. true   false   Before 1992, people in Singapore were careful about where they put gum.

2. true   false   Trains were late because their doors didn't work well.

3. true   false   For more than ten years people went without chewing gum in Singapore.

4. true   false   Dentists think that everyone should give up chewing gum.

5. true   false   You can chew any kind of gum in Singapore now.

Unit 4 Quiz

Name:	Score:	/10 =	%

Part 1: Find the different words

One of the four words is different from the other three. Circle the letter of your choice.

> **Example:** **a.** meat   (**b.**) gum   **c.** bread   **d.** cake
> *You can eat meat, bread, and cake, but you chew gum. You can't eat it.*

1. **a.** afford   **b.** chew   **c.** bite   **d.** taste

2. **a.** inventor   **b.** translator   **c.** tower   **d.** publisher

3. **a.** popular   **b.** successful   **c.** improved   **d.** mistake

4. **a.** tower   **b.** bell   **c.** building   **d.** apartment

5. **a.** figure out   **b.** invent   **c.** improve   **d.** give up

Part 2: Read and answer

Read the passage and decide if the statement is *true* or *false*. Circle your answer.

Some popular places to visit are built by people. Other famous places are created by nature. For example, in the northeast of the United States, there was a famous rock on a high mountain that looked just like an old man. He had lots of hair, a big nose, and a beard. People called him "The Old Man of the Mountain" and every year more than a million people came to look at him. Scientists think that the stone face had been there for about 17,000 years.

In May 2003, there was very bad weather near the Old Man of the Mountain. There were very high winds and the temperature was very cold. The sky was so cloudy that people couldn't see the stone face for many days. As soon as the storm was over, people looked for the Old Man and they couldn't see him. They discovered that he had fallen apart. The stones that made his face sank down the mountain. A number of scientists climbed up to see if they could repair the stone face, but they had to give up. They figured out that the damage from the weather was just too bad.

1. true   false   The Old Man of the Mountain was built by people.

2. true   false   The stone face had a large collar around its neck.

3. true   false   About 17,000 visitors a year saw the Old Man of the Mountain.

4. true   false   During the storm and after it ended, people couldn't see the stone face.

5. true   false   Scientists think high winds and cold caused the Old Man to fall apart.

Unit 5 Quiz

Name:	Score:	/10 =	%

Part 1: Find the same meaning

Decide which words mean the same as the underlined words. Circle your choice.

1. Julie liked her friend's dress so much she <u>made one that looked just like</u> it.

   a. invented   **b.** improved   **c.** discovered   **d.** copied

2. If you stick your fingers into the <u>place where they live</u>, the lions will bite you.

   a. cage   **b.** nest   **c.** tower   **d.** zoo

3. Peter is very tall so he <u>is easily noticed</u> in any group of people.

   a. gives up   **b.** stands out   **c.** takes off   **d.** turns out

4. Carlo got the <u>top award</u> for winning the bicycle race.

   a. best price   **b.** biggest mistake   **c.** first prize   **d.** most success

5. You really have to <u>look after</u> small children when you take them to the zoo.

   a. tell apart   **b.** go without   **c.** take care of   **d.** give up

Part 2: Organize the paragraph

Number the sentences 2–6 in the correct order to make a paragraph.

___7___ Now and then, even birds say the right thing at the right time, even if by accident.

_____ However, copying is not the same thing as thinking what to say on your own.

_____ Perhaps they think this because birds are very intelligent and can copy well.

___1___ Many people think that their pet birds can talk.

_____ Thinking what you are going to say requires a big brain and birds have small brains.

_____ However, without question, they can copy what they hear.

_____ Animals with small brains can't figure out the answers to problems.

Unit 6 Quiz

Name:	Score:	/10 =	%

Part 1: Complete the passage

Use words from the box to complete the passage. Write the words in the spaces. One item is extra.

festivals	belief	celebrate	all of a sudden	at first	around the world

Greeting cards are a popular way to (1)_____ holidays. Often they are sent for birthdays, but

people also send them for (2)_____ such as Christmas or Valentine's Day. Printed cards have

been used for 150 years, but computer greeting cards or "e-cards" have taken off (3)_____.

Some people found it strange (4)_____, but now they send cards that sing and dance on the

computer screen. You can send them (5)_____ with a click of your computer mouse.

Part 2: Read and answer

Read the passage and answer the questions. Circle the letter of the best answer.

In 2000, The British Museum announced they had the oldest Valentine card written in English. They discovered the Valentine message in papers that the museum bought in the 1930s. They showed it to the public in an exhibit on 1,000 years of English literature.

The old Valentine tells an interesting story. In 1477, a woman named Margery Brews sent a Valentine message to John Paston. The two had fallen in love and were engaged to be married. At that time, the woman's family gave money to the man at marriage. John wanted more money than Margery's family could afford. Margery asked her mother to talk to her father about this, but **he** said no. In the Valentine, Margery told John he should love her and protect her. She said that money was not as important as love. It turned out that the story had a happy ending. Margery and John married and lived happily with their two children.

1. The best title for this story is . . .

  a. Two Old Valentines.

  b. Love, Not Money.

  c. John's Love Message.

  d. Love in the Museum.

2. When was the message written?

  a. 2000   **b.** 1000   **c.** 1930   **d.** 1477

3. At the time of the Valentine message, Margery and John . . .

  a. were engaged.

  b. were married.

  c. had two children.

  d. gave each other money.

4. In the second paragraph the word **he** refers to . . .

  a. John Paston.   **b.** John's father.   **c.** Margery's father.   **d.** Valentine.

5. The Valentine message said that . . .

  a. John should take care of Margery.

  b. the family should celebrate.

  c. love wasn't as important as money.

  d. Mary should give up John.

Unit 7 Quiz

Part 1: Find the same meaning

Decide which words mean the same as the underlined words. Circle your choice.

1. My sister loves to read books about <u>things that happened in the past</u>.
   - **a.** beliefs
   - **b.** festivals
   - **c.** history
   - **d.** translation

2. Birds can often be seen standing on the <u>top</u> of a building.
   - **a.** roof
   - **b.** nest
   - **c.** zoo
   - **d.** cage

3. When Martin <u>learned</u> the exam results, he was very happy.
   - **a.** turned out
   - **b.** took part in
   - **c.** gave up
   - **d.** found out

4. Tom Sawyer looked for money and treasure that was <u>put into the ground</u>.
   - **a.** sunken
   - **b.** buried
   - **c.** improved
   - **d.** invented

5. In fairy tales, witches are <u>not kind and hurt other people</u>.
   - **a.** cruel
   - **b.** intelligent
   - **c.** popular
   - **d.** successful

Part 2: Read and answer

Read the news report and decide if the statement is *true*, *false*, or *unknown*. Circle your answer.

End of Taj Tourist Project

Agra, India, June 24 A huge tourist project near the Taj Mahal has been stopped. Workers are not taking part in the 33 million dollar project any more. The shopping mall with shops, restaurants, and cinemas was designed to give visitors everything they needed near the Taj. They would not need to shop in the city of Agra. Now the government has called off all work on the project because it could hurt the famous building.

Shah Jahan built the Taj Mahal 400 years ago as a tomb for his favorite wife. It is beside the Jumna River. Conservationists, people who protect the environment, say that the project would move the river away from the Taj. This would hurt the base or bottom of the famous building. The marble building might fall apart and then tourists would not come to visit it. The Taj Mahal is the most important tourist attraction in India. India's economy would be badly hurt if the Taj is damaged.

---

1. true   false   unknown   Work continues on the Taj Mahal tourist project.

2. true   false   unknown   The project would cost more than $30,000,000.

3. true   false   unknown   Agra city is five miles away from the Taj Mahal.

4. true   false   unknown   Changing the river could make the Taj Mahal fall apart.

5. true   false   unknown   Tourism is the most important part of India's economy.

Unit 8 Quiz

Name:		Score:	/10 =	%

▊ Part 1: Find the different words

One of the four words is different from the other three. Circle the letter of your choice.

Example: **a.** gloves   **b.** collar   **c.** roof   **d.** underwear
You can wear gloves, a collar, and underwear. A roof is part of a building.

1. **a.** sometimes   **b.** off and on   **c.** now and then   **d.** always

2. **a.** cruel   **b.** successful   **c.** a big hit   **d.** lucky

3. **a.** 12 years   **b.** 1990–2003   **c.** at first   **d.** period

4. **a.** sleep   **b.** brain   **c.** dream   **d.** think

5. **a.** find out   **b.** turn out   **c.** discover   **d.** learn

▊ Part 2: Organize the paragraph

Number the sentences 2–6 in the correct order to make a paragraph.

_____ The next day, he went to the race.

___7___ By earning lots of money, John's dreams came true.

_____ Those horses always won the races.

_____ He dreamed about the next day's horse race.

___1___ For a period of twelve years, John Godley had strange dreams.

_____ At the race, he bet on horses that won in his dream.

_____ When his horses won, lucky John got a lot of money.

Unit 9 Quiz

Name:	Score:	/10 =	%

Part 1: Complete the sentences

Decide which words are best for the spaces. Circle the letter of your choice.

1. It's easy to _____ your computer to the Internet.

   a. bet   **b.** turn into   **c.** take care of   **d.** connect

2. Can you _____ that the story about Jennifer Lopez is true?

   a. dream   **b.** prove   **c.** twist   **d.** celebrate

3. Jeff has such a(n) _____ sense of humor. It's hard to understand his jokes.

   a. strange   **b.** intelligent   **c.** sudden   **d.** popular

4. There's rubber on the _____ of playgrounds so children don't get hurt.

   a. roof   **b.** surface   **c.** cage   **d.** band

5. Most people thought Ben was _____ lucky to have won the prize.

   a. stand out   **b.** straight   **c.** kind of   **d.** come true

Part 2: Complete the passage

Use idioms from the box to complete the passage. Write the words in the spaces. Two are extra.

all of a sudden	around the world	as soon as	in other words
at first	as for	by accident	

(1)_____ people make a number of things with paper. (2)_____, they fold paper into shapes. In Japan, people fold paper to make paper birds and flowers. (3)_____, it may seem difficult. (4)_____ you watch someone else, it becomes easier. Then you have to practice yourself to become good at it. (5)_____, you can turn paper into something beautiful. Don't give up! Keep trying and you'll figure it out.

Unit 10 Quiz

Part 1: Complete the passage

Use words from the box to complete the passage. Write the words in the spaces. One word is extra.

terrible	zoo	taste	dangerous	cage	bite

Without question, many animals are (1)_____ and can hurt you if you are not careful. Now and

then, you hear of someone who works at a (2)_____ who is trapped in a (3)_____ by

accident. All of a sudden, a hungry animal could (4)_____ the zookeeper and it could turn into

a (5)_____ problem. Luckily, this kind of thing doesn't happen very often.

Part 2: Read and answer

Read the passage and answer the questions. Circle the letter of the best answer.

Miners work under the earth to collect coal. They have dangerous jobs because occasionally the earth sinks or falls apart. When this happens, miners are trapped underground. They are buried. If they don't have air to breathe, food to eat, and water to drink, they will die. They cannot go without any of these things for long, but the first is the most important. It is difficult to figure out where miners are and reach them in time. Trapped miners dream of being free and don't give up.

In July 2002, nine miners went to work in Pennsylvania. All of a sudden, there was a terrible accident. A wall broke apart and water flooded the area where the miners were working. It came up to their collars. At first, the miners shouted, but no one could hear them. Luckily, people on the surface figured out where the miners were and dug a breathing hole. Later, they gave them messages from their families. Many people took part in helping to save them. After a period of several days, they brought the tired miners to the surface alive.

1. The best title for this story is . . .

   a. A Miner's Accident.   **c.** Dreams Came True.

   b. A Dangerous Job.   **d.** A Cruel Message.

2. Where was the accident?

   a. underground   **b.** on the surface   **c.** underwater   **d.** beside a wall

3. What is most important to trapped miners?

   a. water   **b.** air   **c.** work   **d.** food

4. When people figured out where the miners were, they first gave them . . .

   a. drinking water.   **b.** family messages.   **c.** a loud shout.   **d.** fresh air.

5. The lesson of this story is that you should . . .

   a. not do dangerous work.   **c.** eat a good lunch at work.

   b. never give up hope.   **d.** learn to swim.

Unit 11 Quiz

Name:	Score:	/10 =	%

Part 1: Find the same meaning

Decide which words mean the same as the underlined words. Circle your choice.

1. Sarah likes to <u>exercise</u> at the gym every night.

   a. improve   **b.** lean   **c.** work out   **d.** figure out

2. <u>A number</u> of my friends have cell phones.

   a. Quite a few   **b.** Now and then   **c.** As soon as   **d.** Off and on

3. In his most recent film, Harry played the role of a <u>policeman</u>.

   a. inventor   **b.** cop   **c.** star   **d.** translator

4. Olympic skiers <u>prepare</u> all year. They go wherever they can find snow.

   a. take part in   **b.** connect   **c.** twist   **d.** train

5. Do you remember that <u>situation</u> when Harry Potter found out about his parents?

   a. scene   **b.** apartment   **c.** tower   **d.** festival

Part 2: Organize the paragraph

Number the sentences 3–7 in the correct order to make a paragraph.

_____ When she was 21, Yeoh won a beauty contest and became Miss Malaysia.

___8___ Today Michelle Yeoh is well known to filmgoers around the world.

_____ In 1985, Yeoh became a huge success in the film *Yes, Madam!*

___1___ Michelle Yeoh is famous for her roles in action films.

_____ During the period when she was a beauty queen, Michelle Yeoh made television commercials and started to act in films.

_____ Her films in the 1990s took off as blockbuster hits.

___2___ She was born in 1962 in Malaysia.

_____ As a young girl, she enjoyed watching action films.

Unit 12 Quiz

Name:	Score:	/10 =	%

Part 1: Complete the passage

Think of words to fill the spaces. The first letter of the word is given to you. Try to spell the words correctly.

Before you go abroad to study, you must (1) a_____ or ask for admission. The university will usually ask you to fill out a (2) f_____ or paper with lots of information. Often there is a (3) f_____ which you must pay. Some countries (4) r_____ or say you need a special visa to study there. When you finish your studies, you will (5) g_____. Your family will be proud of you.

Part 2: Read and answer

Read the passage and decide if the statement is *true, false,* or *unknown*. Circle your answer.

Most colleges and universities in English-speaking countries ask new students to take language examinations before they enter. No matter how many exams you have taken in your home country, it's good to prepare for standardized exams like the TOEFL and IELTS. Some students take special classes or they take part in study groups. These students figure out ways to improve their score and avoid making silly mistakes on the exam. Intelligent students don't just depend on luck to be successful. They prove that they can put their education to good use.

1. true   false   unknown   You will probably need to take a language exam before you study in an English-speaking country.

2. true   false   unknown   According to this article, you don't need to do any special preparation for TOEFL if you've taken lots of exams in your home country.

3. true   false   unknown   Some students in Japan take the TOEIC exam.

4. true   false   unknown   Study groups help students get higher scores.

5. true   false   unknown   The writer thinks that luck is what you really need to be successful.

Unit 13 Quiz

Name: _____   Score: ___ **/10 =** _____ **%**

Part 1: Choose the best answer

Choose the best answer for each question. Circle your choice.

1. What are palaces often made out of?

   a. rubber   **b.** gloves   **c.** furniture   **d.** marble

2. How can a guide help you in a strange place? A guide can . . .

   a. stand out.   **c.** show the way.

   b. work out.   **d.** put something to good use.

3. If something happens during a ten-year period, it happens . . .

   a. over time.   **b.** off and on.   **c.** all of a sudden.   **d.** at first.

4. When something you like vanishes so that it doesn't exist anymore, it . . .

   a. graduates.   **b.** disappears.   **c.** ends up.   **d.** twists.

5. Which item is NOT true about deserts?

   a. They're hot and dry.   **c.** They're found around the world.

   b. They have a lot of sand.   **d.** They have many trees.

Part 2: Read and answer

Read the news report and decide if the statement is *true, false,* or *unknown.* Circle your answer.

Palm Islands

Dubai, March 16 The world's largest man-made islands are being built beside the city of Dubai in the Persian Gulf. These islands are in the shape of palm trees. They are so huge you could see them from the moon. The government of Dubai knows that tourists from all over the world will come to enjoy the desert weather. Bridges and a train will connect the islands to Dubai.

The islands are made out of blocks of stone taken from the bottom of the sea. Big ships dig the blocks and then bury them again in the new shape. Over time, beautiful fish will come to live around the islands. Without question, the palm islands will turn into popular places to visit.

1. true   false   unknown   The Palm Islands are ready for tourists now.

2. true   false   unknown   According to the passage, if you were looking at Earth from the moon you would be able to see the islands.

3. true   false   unknown   The islands will be popular with tourists who like cool holidays.

4. true   false   unknown   The hotels on the islands will hold 5,000 people.

5. true   false   unknown   You will have to travel to the islands by boat.

Unit 14 Quiz

Name: Score: /10 =   %

Part 1: Find the different words

One of the four items is different from the other three. Circle the letter of your choice.

1. **a.** break up   **b.** work out   **c.** fall apart   **d.** divorce

2. **a.** made for each other   **b.** fall in love   **c.** match   **d.** different

3. **a.** legal   **b.** romance   **c.** marriage   **d.** date

4. **a.** enter   **b.** start   **c.** get out of   **d.** begin

5. **a.** cave   **b.** palace   **c.** bell tower   **d.** hotel

Part 2: Organize the paragraph

Number the sentences 2–6 in the correct order to make a paragraph.

__7__   Next June, their dream will come true when their families celebrate their marriage.

_____   So they gave up the idea of dating and just remained friends during high school.

_____   However, their parents thought they were too young to date.

_____   While studying at college, they began to spend more time together and started dating.

__1__   Laura and Pete met when they were twelve and it was love at first sight.

_____   On their first day of college, they found out they were in some of the same classes.

_____   When they graduated from high school, they applied to the same university by accident.

Unit 15 Quiz

▮ Part 1: Complete the sentences

Decide which words are best for the spaces. Circle the letter of your choice.

1. There's an exhibition of Monet's paintings in the _____.
   a. tower   **b.** palace   **c.** museum   **d.** portrait

2. That small gold collar with the diamonds is very _____.
   a. terrible   **b.** valuable   **c.** huge   **d.** cruel

3. We're not sure, but a number of men are _____ hidden in the cave.
   a. said to be   **b.** buried   **c.** trapped   **d.** put to good use

4. Guides help museum visitors by _____ them the way around.
   a. matching   **b.** translating   **c.** discovering   **d.** showing

5. Johann Sebastian Bach was one of the most famous musicians _____.
   a. of all time   **b.** all of a sudden   **c.** now and then   **d.** no matter

▮ Part 2: Complete the passage

Use words and idioms from the box to complete the passage. Write the words in the spaces. Three are extra.

prove	took care of	fee	roof	stolen	message	portrait	hidden

Girl with a Pearl Earring is one of the most successful art novels to be published in recent years. It is about a young girl who worked for the famous Dutch painter, Vermeer. The girl (1)_____ the artist's studio and lived under the same (2)_____ with the rest of Vermeer's family. Vermeer's wife had many children and was too busy to help her husband. Vermeer was painting a (3)_____ of a rich lady. He asked the young girl to model for the painting. He told her to wear one of his wife's valuable pearl earrings. By accident, the wife found out and was very angry. She thought that the young girl had (4)_____ her earring. It took many years to (5)_____ that she hadn't taken it without permission.

Unit 16 Quiz

Name: Score: / 10 =   %

Part 1: Find the same meaning

Decide which words mean the same as the underlined words. Circle your choice.

1. There were many wars <u>in ancient history</u>.
   a. now and then   **b.** of all time   **c.** off and on   **d.** long ago

2. This is my grandmother's <u>old</u> recipe.
   a. valuable   **b.** female   **c.** traditional   **d.** required

3. <u>In fact</u>, it is said that Leif Ericsson discovered America long before Columbus did.
   a. As for   **b.** Actually   **c.** No matter   **d.** Suddenly

4. Sometimes salad is <u>given</u> after the main meal.
   a. served   **b.** chewed   **c.** bitten   **d.** tasted

5. Maria is trying to <u>come up with</u> a better computer program.
   a. invent   **b.** celebrate   **c.** steal   **d.** match

Part 2: Read and answer

Read the passage and answer the questions. Circle the letter of the best answer.

> People around the world eat different things for breakfast. However, in some places, what they eat depends on whether it's an ordinary day or whether a special festival is being celebrated. For example, in Belgium and Holland, the everyday breakfast is meat and cheese sandwiches served with strong coffee. On holidays, people have time for pancakes and waffles. Many British people enjoy a full breakfast of meat, eggs, beans, and mushrooms on the weekend. They drink tea with it.
>
> In other countries, people eat the same thing every day, all year round. In China and Thailand, a rice soup called congee is popular at breakfast. Chinese people prefer to drink tea with it. In Latin countries such as Spain and France, people usually have a light breakfast of bread and coffee, even if it's a holiday.

1. The main idea of the first paragraph is that . . .
   a. people eat more on weekends.   **c.** Holland is famous for cheese.
   b. breakfast is different around the world.   **d.** people eat the same thing everyday.

2. Which is NOT part of a traditional British breakfast?
   a. meat   **b.** beans   **c.** mushrooms   **d.** waffles

3. The main idea of the second paragraph is that . . .
   a. people in Spain eat a special breakfast on holidays.   **c.** many people eat the same thing for breakfast every day.
   b. Chinese people drink a lot of tea.   **d.** breakfast is different on holidays.

4. Congee is made out of . . .
   a. rice.   **b.** beans.   **c.** bread.   **d.** cheese.

5. In which countries do most people drink coffee at breakfast?
   a. Holland and England   **c.** Spain and Belgium
   b. China and Thailand   **d.** Belgium and Britain

Unit 17 Quiz

| Name: | | Score: | /10 = | % |

Part 1: Find the different words

One of the four items is different from the other three. Circle the letter of your choice.

1. **a.** mistake   **b.** win   **c.** beat   **d.** score

2. **a.** at first   **b.** enter   **c.** final   **d.** begin

3. **a.** match   **b.** record   **c.** game   **d.** tournament

4. **a.** fight   **b.** play   **c.** come up against   **d.** come up with

5. **a.** now   **b.** history   **c.** ancient   **d.** long ago

Part 2: Complete the passage

Use words and idioms from the box to complete the passage. Write the words in the spaces. Two are extra.

| record | no matter | make it | final | score | tournament | come up against |

Can you imagine what it would be like to (1)_____ your own sister in one tennis

(2)_____ after another? That's what it's like for the talented Williams sisters. Serena and

Venus Williams often (3)_____ all the way to the (4)_____ match and have to play

against each other. They remain good friends (5)_____ who wins.

This page may be photocopied. Thomson Heinle © 2004

Unit 18 Quiz

Name:	Score:	/10 =	%

▌Part 1: Complete the passage

Think of words to fill the spaces. The first letter of the word is given to you. Try to spell the words correctly.

1. Van Gogh was an o_____ artist because he painted in an imaginative way.

2. My cat is very c_____. She is interested in finding out about everything.

3. You can trust Anna. She is very h_____ and always tells the truth.

4. The publishers hope that the new book will be a h_____ and sell many copies.

5. No ice cream for me, thanks. I really need to l_____ weight.

▌Part 2: Read and answer

Read the passage and decide if the statement is *true, false,* or *unknown.* Circle your answer.

People inherit their blood type from their parents. If both parents have the same blood type, the baby will have that type too. If parents have different blood types, the baby will have the one that is dominant. In biology, *dominant* means the type that is stronger than the other type, which is called *recessive.*

In addition to the four blood types, blood is also classified as Rh positive or Rh negative. Once in a while, a baby will look blue at birth because it has a different Rh from its mother. Doctors have to quickly carry out a transfusion so the baby has blood that is good for it. If this goes well, the baby's skin will change to the normal color and the baby will be healthy.

1. true   false   unknown   If both your parents have type O blood, you can have type B.

2. true   false   unknown   When parents have different blood types, the baby will have the dominant one.

3. true   false   unknown   Blood is only classified into the four types.

4. true   false   unknown   "Blue babies" are often born to young mothers.

5. true   false   unknown   Doctors give the mothers of "blue babies" a transfusion.

Unit 19 Quiz

| Name: | | Score: | /10 = | % |

Part 1: Find the different words

One of the four items is different from the other three. Circle the letter of your choice.

1. **a.** generous   **b.** honest   **c.** curious   **d.** cruel
2. **a.** carry out   **b.** give up   **c.** perform   **d.** do
3. **a.** take off   **b.** be a hit   **c.** fall apart   **d.** go well
4. **a.** war   **b.** murder   **c.** accident   **d.** tournament
5. **a.** attempt   **b.** allow   **c.** permit   **d.** let

Part 2: Read and answer

Read the advertisement and answer the questions. Write the answers in the spaces.

Give Your TV a Break! Annual TV-Turnoff Week March 20–March 27

Join 2.5 million families who will have time to do these things together this week:

take a walk   *go to a soccer match*

visit the zoo or a museum

listen to music   *talk about their dreams*

read a book out loud

**If you want to take part, telephone 609-4377 or fax the form to 609-3744 before March 18th!
There's no fee to register your family.**

---

1. What is the final date of the TV-Turnoff event? _____
2. About how many people will take part, if each family has four people? _____
3. What can families talk about? _____
4. What number do you call to fax the form? _____
5. How much money does it cost to register? _____

This page may be photocopied. Thomson Heinle © 2004

Unit 20 Quiz

Name: Score: /10 =   %

Part 1: Find the same meaning

Decide which words mean the same as the underlined words. Circle your choice.

1. I need to get a new <u>seat</u> for my horse.

   a. roof   **b.** saddle   **c.** recipe   **d.** portrait

2. The <u>contest</u> will happen next weekend.

   a. celebrate   **b.** event   **c.** effect   **d.** attempt

3. Could you help me <u>join together</u> the ribbon on this birthday present, please?

   a. rope   **b.** allow   **c.** tie   **d.** murder

4. In parts of Arabia, it stays dry and without rain <u>for the whole year</u>.

   a. of all time   **b.** now and then   **c.** off and on   **d.** all year round

5. Students come to this university from <u>around the world</u>.

   a. all over   **b.** on the go   **c.** quite a few   **d.** application forms

Part 2: Complete the passage

Use words and idioms from the box to complete the passage. Write the words in the spaces. Three are extra.

no matter how	show off	around the world	without question
all of a sudden	at first	kind of	long ago

(1)_____ there were no rodeos. Then in the 1800s, cowboys in Arizona came up with competitions to prove their skills. (2)_____ these shows were just for the cowboys themselves. Later, the public was invited to attend for a fee. The idea quickly took off and, (3)_____, rodeos were taking place all over the United States. The idea of rodeos then became popular (4)_____. Today, people in many countries are able to see horse riders (5)_____ their amazing skills.

Unit Quizzes Answer Key

For general guidelines on promoting good test-taking strategies, see pages 10–11. Note that true *is abbreviated as* T, *false as* F, *and* unknown *as* U *in the answer key.*

Unit 1

Part 1: 1. popular; **2.** bite; **3.** collar; **4.** zoo;
5. tell apart
Part 2: 1. F; **2.** T; **3.** F; **4.** F; **5.** T

Unit 2

Part 1: 1. successful; **2.** go without; **3.** apartment;
4. took off; **5.** without question
Part 2: 1. c; **2.** a; **3.** b; **4.** c; **5.** d

Unit 3

Part 1: 1. d; **2.** c; **3.** b; **4.** c; **5.** a
Part 2: 1. F; **2.** T; **3.** T; **4.** F; **5.** F

Unit 4

Part 1: 1. a; **2.** c; **3.** d; **4.** b; **5.** d
Part 2: 1. F; **2.** F; **3.** F; **4.** T; **5.** T

Unit 5

Part 1: 1. d; **2.** a; **3.** b; **4.** c; **5.** c
Part 2: 7; 3; 2; 1; 4; 6; 5 order

Unit 6

Part 1: 1. celebrate; **2.** festivals; **3.** all of a sudden;
4. at first; **5.** around the world
Part 2: 1. b; **2.** d; **3.** a; **4.** c; **5.** a

Unit 7

Part 1: 1. c; **2.** a; **3.** d; **4.** b; **5.** a
Part 2: 1. F; **2.** T; **3.** U; **4.** T; **5.** U

Unit 8

Part 1: 1. d; **2.** a; **3.** c; **4.** b; **5.** b
Part 2: 3; 7; 5; 2; 1; 4; 6 order

Unit 9

Part 1: 1. d; **2.** b; **3.** a; **4.** b; **5.** c
Part 2: 1. Around the world; **2.** In other words;
3. At first; **4.** As soon as; **5.** All of a sudden

Unit 10

Part 1: 1. dangerous; **2.** zoo; **3.** cage; **4.** bite;
5. terrible
Part 2: 1. b; **2.** a; **3.** b; **4.** d; **5.** b

Unit 11

Part 1: 1. c; **2.** a; **3.** b; **4.** d; **5.** a
Part 2: 4; 8; 6; 1; 5; 7; 2; 3 order

Unit 12

Part 1: 1. apply; **2.** form; **3.** fee; **4.** require;
5. graduate
Part 2: 1. T; **2.** F; **3.** U; **4.** T; **5.** F

Unit 13

Part 1: 1. d; **2.** c; **3.** a; **4.** b; **5.** d
Part 2: 1. F; **2.** T; **3.** F; **4.** U; **5.** F

Unit 14

Part 1: 1. b; **2.** d; **3.** a; **4.** c; **5.** a
Part 2: 7; 3; 2; 6; 1; 5; 4 order

Unit 15

Part 1: 1. c; **2.** b; **3.** a; **4.** d; **5.** a
Part 2: 1. took care of; **2.** roof; **3.** portrait;
4. stolen; **5.** prove

Unit 16

Part 1: 1. d; **2.** c; **3.** b; **4.** a; **5.** a
Part 2: 1. b; **2.** d; **3.** c; **4.** a; **5.** c

Unit 17

Part 1: 1. a; **2.** c; **3.** b; **4.** d; **5.** a
Part 2: 1. come up against; **2.** tournament;
3. make it; **4.** final; **5.** no matter

Unit 18

Part 1: 1. original; **2.** curious; **3.** honest; **4.** hit;
5. lose
Part 2: 1. F; **2.** T; **3.** F; **4.** U; **5.** F

Unit 19

Part 1: 1. d; **2.** b; **3.** c; **4.** d; **5.** a
Part 2: 1. March 27; **2.** 10 million; **3.** dreams;
4. 609-3744; **5.** nothing (it's free)

Unit 20

Part 1: 1. b; **2.** b; **3.** c; **4.** d; **5.** a
Part 2: 1. Long ago; **2.** At first; **3.** all of a sudden;
4. around the world; **5.** show off

Introduction to Tests

This section contains two tests—a mid-book test covering Units 1–10, and a final test covering the whole book. Each test contains fifty questions over four pages, and is expected to take about an hour. The test answer key is provided on page 76, and each question is worth two points, for a total mark out of a hundred.

Tests are divided into four sections.

▉ Part 1: Vocabulary (25 questions)

These follow the format of the corresponding activity type in the unit quizzes (see page 45).

a. Match the words and definitions. (10 questions)

b. Find the different words. (5 questions)

c. Find the same meaning. (10 questions)

▉ Part 2: Complete the passage (5 questions)

This is a cloze passage where students find the items to fill five gaps in a passage.

▉ Part 3: Read and answer (10 questions)

a. Read the passage and decide if the statement is true, false, or unknown. (5 questions)

b. Circle the letter of the best answer. (5 questions)

▉ Part 4: Scan for information (10 questions)

In this part there are a number of short "classified ad" type readings and students are required to scan these for information to answer ten short-answer questions.

For convenience in keeping track of students' scores on the tests, as well as the unit quizzes, a photocopiable scoring sheet is provided on page 77.

Mid-book Test

Name: Score: /50 =   %

■ Part 1: Vocabulary

A. Match the words and definitions

Find the word for each definition in the box. Write the word on the line next to the definition. Three words are extra.

shout	dream	female	period	rubber	tired	race
message	festival	straight	surface	bell	collar	

1. _____ in a line and not to one side or the other

2. _____ soft material used to make tires and balls

3. _____ metal object that makes a nice sound when you ring it

4. _____ length of time, like the 1990s or a century

5. _____ a happy time when people celebrate

6. _____ a contest to see who is the fastest

7. _____ things you see while you sleep

8. _____ to speak or yell very loudly

9. _____ the top of something

10. _____ sleepy or weak

B. Find the different words

One of the four items is different from the other three. Circle the letter of your choice.

11. **a.** terrible   **b.** dangerous   **c.** cruel   **d.** successful

12. **a.** marble   **b.** gloves   **c.** collar   **d.** underwear

13. **a.** twist   **b.** beside   **c.** lean   **d.** sink

14. **a.** shout   **b.** bite   **c.** bury   **d.** chew

15. **a.** earn   **b.** money   **c.** win   **d.** afford

C. Find the same meaning

Decide which words mean the same as the <u>underlined</u> words. Circle your choice.

16. People wanted Galileo to <u>show that it was true</u> that the Earth went around the Sun.

    a. believe   **b.** prove   **c.** improve   **d.** translate

17. It's <u>a little bit</u> cruel to make horses race twice in one day.

    a. kind of   **b.** off and on   **c.** without question   **d.** by accident

18. I feel terrible because I think I wrote a <u>wrong answer</u> on the exam.

    a. message   **b.** copy   **c.** dream   **d.** mistake

19. Fran is very <u>clever</u> and learns new things quickly.

    a. successful   **b.** popular   **c.** intelligent   **d.** lucky

20. At races, it's difficult to <u>see the differences between</u> the runners without numbers.

    a. fall apart   **b.** stand out   **c.** tell apart   **d.** take care of

21. How do I <u>put together</u> a hands-free headset with my cell phone?

    a. lean   **b.** improve   **c.** stand out   **d.** connect

22. Underwear is on the third floor. You can walk up the stairs or take the <u>lift</u>.

    a. elevator   **b.** surface   **c.** tower   **d.** roof

23. David <u>learned</u> about the race in the newspaper.

    a. found out   **b.** took off   **c.** won   **d.** fell apart

24. It was raining when Sandy <u>entered</u> the taxi.

    a. started   **b.** got in   **c.** discovered   **d.** got out of

25. Dick's parrot won the top <u>award</u> as the best bird in the show.

    a. nest   **b.** bet   **c.** prize   **d.** cage

Part 2: Complete the passage

Use words from the box to complete the passage. Write the words in the spaces. One item is extra.

turned into	as for	as soon as	come true	in other words	dangerous

Andy Lee won't forget last April 17. The day got off to a bad start when he was late to work and had to drive fast. (26)_____ he got on the main highway, Andy saw a dark cloud. Within minutes the cloud (27)_____ a strange funnel shape. (28)_____, Andy knew the cloud was a (29)_____ storm called a tornado, or twister. He remembered he should get off the road and find a place to hide. Luckily, the storm passed beside him and didn't hurt him at all. (30)_____ being late to work, Andy's boss was happy that he got there safely.

New York, August 17 Kim Jones planned a birthday party for her boyfriend Sam Phillips last Thursday night after work. However, the evening turned out differently than either of them had expected. In the late afternoon a huge electricity blackout hit seven northeastern states and three provinces in Canada. Just after four o'clock, a time when millions of people leave their offices and head home, the electricity stopped, so elevators and the subway systems in large cities like New York and Toronto didn't work. Flights could not land or take off at major airports. As soon as most people found out about the blackout, they put their cell phones to good use and called their families to let them know where they were.

Kim works on the 70th floor of an apartment tower in New York. She had just left her office and was trapped in an elevator on the 65th floor. At first she was worried. She called Sam and discovered what had happened. He told her not to give up hope. Then Sam remembered that his friend Joe also worked high in that building. Joe could take care of the situation. About five o'clock, Joe and some other workers figured out that they could get Kim out of the elevator through its roof. Kim still ended up having to walk down a lot of stairs, but that wasn't so terrible. Kim felt tired, but she also felt lucky. When she got down to the street at eight o'clock, she found Sam waiting for her. A number of their friends were there too. As for the birthday party, it turned into a picnic by candlelight because the city went without electricity for several days. Sam said he'd never forget it.

A. Read the passage and decide if the statement is *true, false,* or *unknown*. Circle your answer.

31. true false unknown A *blackout* means it is dark, without electric lights.

32. true false unknown People in seven northwestern states had a problem.

33. truc false unknown Elevators and subways did not run, but airports worked as usual.

34. true false unknown Kim works for a publisher on the 70th floor of the tower.

35. true false unknown Kim had to walk down 65 floors of stairs.

B. Now circle the letter of the best answer.

36. The best title for this passage is . . .

    a. Dark Night in Toronto.   **c.** A Change in Plans.

    b. The Long Walk Home.   **d.** Trapped in the Subway.

37. Many people finish work at . . .

    a. 3 p.m.   **b.** 4 p.m.   **c.** 5 p.m.   **d.** 7 p.m.

38. When did people call their families?

    a. at five o'clock   **c.** at eight o'clock

    b. before the blackout   **d.** just after the blackout

39. How did Kim feel in the beginning?

    a. worried   **b.** tired   **c.** lucky   **d.** terrible

40. Which one is NOT true?

    a. Some friends came to the party.   **c.** Sam forgot his birthday.

    b. The party started after eight.   **d.** There was no electricity that night.

Part 4: Scan for information

Read the question and figure out what you need to know. Then quickly look at the advertisements and find the answer. Write a short answer in the space.

41. Where can you see historical pictures of India? _____

42. How many steps are there to the top of the tower? _____

43. When does the live music for the dance start? _____

44. Are the safari animals in cages? _____

45. What is "intelligent" at the Magic Show? _____

46. What can you make at the Children's Museum? _____

47. If two people go to the dance as a couple, how much money will they save? _____

48. What building is on the same street as the City Art Museum? _____

49. When does the Magic Show end? _____

50. Can a family climb the bell tower on Saturday? _____

COMING SOON

ROMANTIC DANCE

Celebrate a special date or anniversary

Bring your sweetheart

Saturday night
live band 9 p.m. – 1 a.m.
Country Club
$25 a couple
$15 for one person

AFRICAN SAFARI PARK
A Drive-through Zoo

Drive in your own car or take the special train

See lions, giraffes, zebras, and elephants without cages

Open every day 9–4
Special family tickets
$35 for 4 people

HARRY POTTER
MAGIC SHOW

See magic tricks
• the quiet bell
• the intelligent ball
• the terrible message

• two full hours •
• Saturday morning •
• starts at 9:30 •
• The Grand Cinema 741 High Street •

THE TAJ

100 years of pictures
THEN AND NOW
See the Taj in history from
1900 to 2000

Photography Exhibit

February 1 – April 30

City Art Museum 750 High Street

Tuesday to Sunday 10 a.m. to 5 p.m.

BELL TOWER
TOURS

Great view from the top!

Climb 439 steps or take the elevator

Learn the 300-year history of our city

Sundays only • 8 a.m. to 3 p.m.
No children under 8

CHILDREN'S MUSEUM

Special Show on Inventors in History

• **Make a Mobius Band**
• **Figure out a puzzle**

February 15 – March 15
For children 5 and over
and their parents
Open every day except Wednesday
8–4

Final Test

Part 1: Vocabulary

A. Match the words and definitions

Find the word for each definition in the box. Write the word on the line next to the definition. Three words are extra.

guide	cop	beat	earn	gloves	cave	role
desert	message	form	improve	allow	match	

1. _____ clothing you wear to keep your hands warm

2. _____ make something better

3. _____ get money or a college degree by working hard

4. _____ things or people that go well together

5. _____ a part played by an actor or actress

6. _____ information given in a short note or spoken

7. _____ an informal way of talking about a policeman

8. _____ let or permit

9. _____ a paper with questions that you can fill out

10. _____ do better than or win against

B. Find the different words

One of the four items is different from the other three. Circle the letter of your choice.

11. **a.** female   **b.** male   **c.** girl   **d.** woman

12. **a.** required   **b.** popular   **c.** outgoing   **d.** well-liked

13. **a.** cage   **b.** zoo   **c.** nest   **d.** tower

14. **a.** final   **b.** end up   **c.** at first   **d.** last

15. **a.** train   **b.** give up   **c.** prepare   **d.** get ready

C. Find the same meaning

Decide which words mean the same as the <u>underlined</u> words. Circle your choice.

16. I can't <u>pay that much money for</u> a new computer.

    a. earn   **b.** make   **c.** afford   **d.** bet

17. That TV show was <u>sent over the air</u> for the first time in 1987.

    a. a hit   **b.** broadcast   **c.** turned out   **d.** published

18. Everyone at their wedding thought that Susan and Pete make a great married <u>pair</u>.

    a. couple   **b.** divorce   **c.** love   **d.** date

19. Christmas is a <u>happy event</u> that people celebrate on December 25.

    a. festival   **b.** belief   **c.** program   **d.** scene

20. My aunt Lucy is very kind and <u>loves to give presents</u>.

    a. stands out   **b.** original   **c.** cruel   **d.** generous

21. I can't find my favorite CD. Where did you <u>put it so I can't find</u> it?

    a. record   **b.** steal   **c.** serve   **d.** hide

22. Tom won a big prize in the competition. He always has such <u>good things happen to him</u>.

    a. recipes   **b.** luck   **c.** dreams   **d.** accidents

23. The team got all the way to the final <u>game</u> in the tournament before they were beaten.

    a. wrestle   **b.** war   **c.** match   **d.** competition

24. Television stations have to pay attention to the opinions of the <u>people in the area</u>.

    a. cops   **b.** visitors   **c.** inventors   **d.** public

25. Michelle Yeoh <u>had an important role</u> in the film *Crouching Tiger, Hidden Dragon*.

    a. starred   **b.** went well   **c.** worked out   **d.** showed the way

Part 2: Complete the passage

Use words from the box to complete the passage. Write the words in the spaces. One item is extra.

made out of	no matter where	turn my attention	actually	going without	put it to

Without question, my cell phone is my favorite item. I cannot dream of (26)_____ it
for even one day. (27)_____, I could (28)_____ better use if I learned
to send and get text messages. That way, I wouldn't have to (29)_____ to my cell
phone every time I get a call. (30)_____ I travel, I always have it with me.

Part 3: Read and answer

One of the great questions of all time still has scientists taking part in discussions: What happened to the land called Atlantis? Long ago, the ancient Greek philosopher Plato said that Atlantis was a beautiful land near Europe. Historians believed that it was a very wealthy place with palaces and traditional culture. All of a sudden it disappeared. Ancient people thought it sank into the sea. Over time, a number of scientists have attempted to look for it, but they have always given up because they haven't found anything.

Now, some scientists believe that the Greek island of Santorini may be the lost Atlantis. Today, Santorini is a circular island in the Aegean Sea with a huge hole in the center filled with sea water. However, 3,500 years ago it looked very different. Then it was a round island with a tall volcano in the middle. Today, Santorini has thirteen villages and about 6,000 people, but in the past it had cities and perhaps even more people. Starting in 1967, archaeologists (scientists who study old things from the earth) started to carry out a big dig on Santorini. They were curious about what was underground. They found part of a city with apartment buildings full of furniture as well as streets and water systems. They also found quite a few colored paintings and portraits on the walls of houses. They showed what the people did every day. Young men fished and young women gathered lovely flowers. The pictures show a peaceful scene. In 1999, the **diggers** discovered some valuable gold art showing a female calf.

Archaeologists figured out that this city beside the sea was buried by a terrible explosion of the volcano. Hot lava and ash suddenly came out of the volcano and buried the roofs of the city. To this date, scientists have not found the bodies of any people trapped there. They think that in the final days before the volcano blew the island apart, the people were successfully able to get out. Although Santorini is said to be the lost Atlantis, no one has proved it yet. Today tourists from around the world come to see the museum and wonder if Santorini is actually the lost Atlantis. Without question, it is a very beautiful place despite its strange history.

A. Read the passage and decide if the statement is *true, false,* or *unknown*. Circle your answer.

31. true   false   unknown   In the past, people believed that Atlantis sank into the sea.

32. true   false   unknown   At first, the attempts to find Atlantis were successful.

33. true   false   unknown   Today Santorini has a volcano in its center.

34. true   false   unknown   The paintings were painted by young children.

35. true   false   unknown   Santorini is popular with visitors from all over.

B. Now circle the letter of the best answer.

36. The best title for this passage is . . .

    a. Greek Islands.   **b.** A Famous Volcano.   **c.** An Ancient Museum.   **d.** Has Atlantis Been Found?

37. In the last sentence of the second paragraph, **<u>diggers</u>** means . . .

    a. young men.   **b.** young women.   **c.** archaeologists.   **d.** artists.

38. The dangerous volcanic event took place . . .

    a. in 1967   **b.** 3,500 years ago.   **c.** 6,000 years ago.   **d.** The passage doesn't say.

39. What was the effect of the volcanic event?

    a. The ancient city was buried.   **c.** The museum disappeared.

    b. Many people were murdered.   **d.** Visitors from around the world were trapped.

40. What was NOT found in the dig?

    a. furniture   **b.** portraits   **c.** water systems   **d.** a golden collar

Part 4: Scan for information

Read the question and figure out what you need to know. Then quickly look at the advertisements and find the answer. Write a short answer in the space.

41. What time is the final soccer game? _____

42. What number do you call for soccer information? _____

43. What can you win at the rodeo? _____

44. What film star can you see on Saturday night? _____

45. Who can NOT go to the horse races? _____

46. How much money can you save at Grandview Mall? _____

47. When can you get ready for exams? _____

48. How much does it cost to apply to the community college? _____

49. What can children do on Saturday morning? _____

50. Can you walk to the horse races from the city center? _____

COMMUNITY EVENTS

||||| SOCCER TOURNAMENT |||||

Final Match Sunday
— **2 p.m.** —

Will the local team make it all the way to the end?

Find out more by calling
— **368-6061** —

Traditional RODEO ★

★ *One day only- Saturday*

Enter the competition for best cowboy prize and get a valuable saddle.

Children's show Saturday at 10 a.m.

HORSE RACING
ALL YEAR ROUND

- Races at 3 p.m.
- Every Sunday
- Only 20 miles away
- Lots of free parking
- No children allowed

VALENTINE'S DAY BIG SALE

Friday 6–9 p.m.
EVERYTHING 20–40% OFF

Make your dreams come true and save time and money.

Visit us at Block G, Grandview Mall.

Fall in love with prices you can afford.

BIG HITS CINEMA
Monday to Saturday

Films every night at 7

Actress of the week:
Michelle Yeoh

Harry Potter children's show Saturday at 2 p.m.

EXAM PREPARATION
APPLY NOW –no fee

- ✐ Classes weeknights
- ✐ 7–9 p.m.
- ✐ Marble Building, Central Community College
- ✐ Parking and child care on site

Tests Answer Key

Mid-book Test

Part 1: Vocabulary
A. 1. straight; 2. rubber; 3. bell; 4. period; 5. festival; 6. race; 7. dream; 8. shout; 9. surface; 10. tired;
B. 11. d; 12. a; 13. b; 14. c; 15. b;
C. 16. b; 17. a; 18. d; 19. c; 20. c; 21. d; 22. a; 23. a; 24. b; 25. c

Part 2: Complete the passage
26. As soon as; 27. turned into; 28. In other words; 29. dangerous; 30. As for

Part 3: Read and answer
A. 31. true; 32. false; 33. unknown; 34. unknown; 35. true;
B. 36. c; 37. b; 38. d; 39. a; 40. c

Part 4: Scan for information
41. City Art Museum; 42. 439; 43. 9 p.m.; 44. no; 45. a ball; 46. a Mobius band; 47. $5;
48. The Grand Cinema; 49. 11:30 a.m.; 50. no

Each item counts two points for a score of 100%.

Final Test

Part 1: Vocabulary
A. 1. gloves; 2. improve; 3. earn; 4. match; 5. role; 6. message; 7. cop; 8. allow; 9. form; 10. beat;
B. 11. b; 12. a; 13. d; 14. c; 15. b;
C. 16. c; 17. b; 18. a; 19. a; 20. d; 21. d; 22. b; 23. c; 24. d; 25. a

Part 2: Complete the passage
26. going without; 27. Actually; 28. put it; 29. turn my attention; 30. No matter where

Part 3: Read and answer
A. 31. true; 32. false; 33. false; 34. unknown; 35. true;
B. 36. d; 37. c; 38. b; 39. a; 40. d

Part 4: Scan for information
41. Sunday at 2 p.m.; 42. 368-6061; 43. a (valuable) saddle; 44. Michelle Yeoh; 45. children;
46. Valentine Sale; 47. weeknights 7–9 p.m.; 48. nothing (it's free); 49. rodeo (children's show); 50. no

Each item counts two points for a score of 100%.

Score Sheet

Class:	Unit Quizzes																				Tests	
Student Name	1	2	3	4	5	6	7	8	9	10	11	12	13	14	15	16	17	18	19	20	mid	final

Glossary

Here are some words that you'll find often in the *Reading Advantage* series, and some other words related to reading and vocabulary acquisition. Understanding these words will help you gain more from the series.

affixes	parts that are attached to the beginning (**prefix**) and end (**suffix**) of a word that change the meaning or the part of speech. The word that results is called a **derivative**, meaning it came from a **root** or **base word**.
antonyms	words with opposite meanings, e.g., tall – short, up – down
background	what learners already know about a subject. **Pre-reading** activities help students to use their background knowledge of a topic.
base word	another word for **root**. For example, *dangerous* has the base word *danger*.
bilingual	**bilingual** dictionaries translate meanings from one language to another (see **monolingual**)
compound word	a word formed from two or more **root** words. Examples of compound words: *bus stop, fireplace, rocking chair*.
connotation	additional meanings a word has besides its central meaning (**denotation**). For example, *spinster* has the meaning of "an unmarried woman," but it has the connotation of an older woman, and many young unmarried women would find it strange to be called a spinster.
content words	words that carry meaning when the word is used alone, such as nouns, verbs, adjectives, and adverbs (see **function words**)
cloze	a classroom activity or testing format where some words are left out and replaced by blanks. You can make a cloze by leaving out every *n*th word (every seventh word, for example) or only certain kinds of words such as verbs or current vocabulary items.
collocations	words that are often found together, for example *commit murder,* or *carry out research,* or *perform surgery*
definition	the meaning of a word
denotation	the central meaning of the word (see **connotation**)
derivative	a word formed by adding a **prefix** or **suffix**
ellipsis	leaving out words from the text that are understood in the context, for example "Mary went shopping last weekend, but Jill didn't (go shopping)." (see **reference, substitution**)
formal	language that you would use in a professional or work situation (with a superior), rather than with friends (see **informal**)
function words	words which have little meaning alone, but are used to show grammatical relationships, such as pronouns (*she, he, they*), articles (*a, an, the*), and conjunctions (*and, but, so*)
gist	the general meaning of a reading passage
homonyms	words that look the same but mean something different. *Polish* (meaning from Poland) and *polish* (to shine) have different meanings.

homophones	words that sound the same but are spelled differently. *Red* the color sounds just like *read*, the past tense verb. Note that *read* has two different sounds, depending on whether the verb is present or past tense.
idiom	a group of words that means something as a group that differs from the meanings of the individual words, such as *keep an eye on, put up with, over the moon*
inference	figuring out what is meant in a reading by going beyond just what the words say
informal	language you would use with people you feel comfortable with, such as close friends or family (see **formal**)
lexis	the vocabulary of a language (rather than grammar)
mental lexicon	the way words are stored in the brain so they can be used and connected with other words or ideas
monolingual	literally, "one language," used for English-English dictionaries. See **bilingual**.
mnemonics	memory aids
nonlinear	a reading passage that isn't prose, for example, timetables and advertisements.
post-reading	done after students have read the passage. See **pre-reading**.
prediction	saying what you think is going to happen before you read a passage
prefix	a letter or group of letters that are added to the beginning of a word to change the meaning of the word, for example, *pre-, post-, un-, ex-* (see **affix, suffix**)
pre-reading	done before students have read the passage (see **background, post-reading**)
reference	using pronouns to refer to people, things, or events that were mentioned in another place in the text, for example, "John took the cup and put **it** on the table." (see **ellipsis, substitution**)
recycling	using a vocabulary item again. Research shows that students don't remember vocabulary unless they have to use the items over and over.
root	the basic part of a word, which may appear on its own (*danger, color, take, fire*) or may take **affixes** (*dangerous, colorful, retake*) or form a **compound word** (*fireplace, fireman*)
scanning	looking quickly at a text for specific information such as dates or facts
skimming	looking quickly at a text to get the **gist** or general meaning
substitution	the use of a word to take the place of the thing being discussed, for example, "I don't want that pen, I want the other **one**." (see **ellipsis, reference**)
suffix	a letter or group of letters that are added to the end of a word to change the meaning of the word, e.g., *-er, -est, -ization, -ful* (see **prefix, affix**)
synonyms	words or idioms that have a similar meaning. Note that *similar* and *same* are different. For example, some words are more formal than others. Some synonyms have different **connotations**.
syllables	the smallest sound units of words. Dictionaries show syllables, e.g., *caterpillar* has four syllables: *cat·er·pil·lar.*

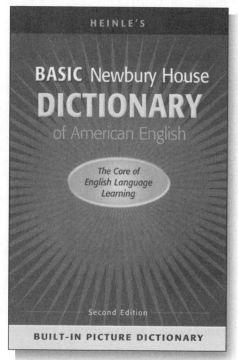
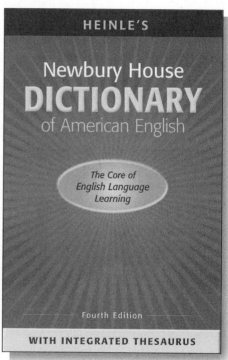